CHANGE WIZARD

MASTER THE ART OF LEADING CHANGE AND WORKING TOGETHER FOR A COMMON PURPOSE

MARLENE GONZALEZ

LIFE COACHING GROUP LLC

Hard Cover ISBN # 978-1-956253-05-4

Paper Back ISBN: 978-1-7371917-0-4

Audiobook ISBN: 978-1-7371917-1-1

Ebook ISBN: ISBN: 978-1-7371917-2-8

CONTENTS

This book is dedicated to every person of any race or age who dreams of unlocking the leader in him or her. The next generation of leaders – on your shoulders lays the responsibility to build a better world.

This book is dedicated to my husband, Carlos – you are my rock and thought partner. Thanks for your love and support. My sister, Vanessa, for her unconditional support in making my dream to write this series of coaching eBooks possible.

This book is also dedicated to Hispanic Alliance for Career Enhancement, HACE. A big thanks to my alumni, clients, coaches, partners and mentors. Additionally, my nieces and nephews. I would like to give you an additional edge, as some of you are just starting your professional journey. To my publishing team – Nick, Myra, Kevin, Susan, Dwinny, AIA Team and Sarah at Publishing Life Services – you are awesome.

JOIN OUR COMMUNITY

Please, don't make the journey alone.

In order to maximize your investment in this book, I encourage you to join our support community on our website www.marlenegonzalez.com.

It is a support group where to share and learn leadership experience and valuable content. We often host free book/audiobook giveaways and helpful resources that will be key to your leadership journey.

It will be great to connect with you there,

Your coach, Marlene Gonzalez

"One of the only ways to get out of a tight box is to invent your way out."

— JEFF BEZOS

INTRODUCTION

Change is one of those things that often frightens or confuses people. Deep down, we all know that change is a normal part of life. However, when you have developed a comfort zone, there's a tendency to resist anything that threatens to disrupt it. As a result, you sometimes hesitate to make a long-overdue change. At other times, you start the change process but somehow fail to see it through. Indeed, managing change requires a lot of commitment and persistence on top of having the right strategies.

Whether you want to transform your organization or simply make a personal change, there's one thing you cannot escape. Change must begin with you. You must be prepared to adjust your mindset because it is the source of resistance to change. If you cannot overcome the resistance in your own mind, you will not succeed in adopting or driving change in your organization. The same applies if you're in a position of leadership.

Any leadership position requires you to be willing and able to challenge certain norms that have been accepted in the organization. Resistance comes from an inability to question the status quo. Once you've dealt with your own resistance, you must help others overcome theirs. This is because implementing change is a team effort.

A leader cannot implement change alone. In chess, the king is the most valuable piece, and the queen is the most powerful. However, the two are useless without the army of pawns standing on the front lines. Therefore, you must also help adjust the mindset of the people around you so that everyone can work together for a common purpose.

But this is often easier said than done. Let me ask you, "Which category of people in an organization is most likely to resist change?" If you answered, "front-line employees," you'd be wrong. Contrary to popular opinion, they are not the most resistant to transformational change. It's the middle to upper levels of management. But why is this so?

To answer this question, you must consider who has the most to lose in an organization during periods of transition. In such instances, the greatest level of resistance usually comes from those who are afraid of losing power and prestige. Those who resist the most are individuals who have the greatest interest in maintaining the status quo. In almost every organization, they are in the upper layers of management. The level of resistance is often directly proportional to the level of disruption the change will create.

The need for change never goes away. You should accept that change is constant. In most cases, if you refuse to acknowledge this fact, you'll never grow or learn your lessons. You don't want to be one of those leaders who fight against a change when the time has come. Such leaders always end up on the wrong side of history — disillusioned and dejected. But what does this mean for you?

Think of a circus juggler in action. They are supposed to toss objects in the air and keep them from falling to the ground. A good juggler has the magical ability to comfortably handle several objects at the same time without dropping a single one. As a leader, you must also learn how to balance several activities competing for your attention. There is a lot that goes into change management. You have to juggle tight deadlines, resource prioritization, communication with stakeholders, and office politics. As you do all this, you still need to preserve crucial relationships with people in your organization.

Maybe you're a senior manager, director, or chief officer trying to execute small changes within your team or even large-scale changes to your organization. You could be a business student or professor interested in management theories. Whatever role you are playing, you need to understand that change is not only inevitable but necessary. Without change, people and systems stagnate, and an organization may lose its dynamism.

If you're reading this book, maybe you've realized the need for changes in your organization. You can see the effect that these changes would have on employees and your work processes. However, you don't understand why this change doesn't happen. You probably wonder why fellow peers, executives, or senior management don't see the need for changing things to improve workplace conditions and output.

Maybe you've overcome the first hurdle in the change process, and the decision has already been made to implement change within your organization. Great! But now you're facing a different challenge. Let's say that you are new to the organization and are inheriting a change initiative. How do you lead this change?

Here is a fact you'll have to deal with. Executing changes, in general, is hard enough. Like a juggler, you deal with so many moving parts — different personalities with egos to protect and multiple systems to reorganize. But imagine if you're trying to execute large-scale changes throughout an organization. This can be an overwhelming process, and most leaders often struggle to figure out how to go about it. You should surround yourself with people who understand not just the theory of change management but the practical aspects of it.

If you somehow manage to come up with a solid plan on how to change things, you should be prepared for resistance. When you have a large number of people who are used to working in a specific way, it becomes exceedingly difficult to try to change their thinking or environment. Employees are known to resist changes in their workplace, especially if they feel that they were not consulted. They may also resist if they feel that the changes threaten their livelihood and ability to be productive. Sometimes, the resistance may come from top management, and it isn't unusual for executives to sabotage changes within their organizations. Dealing with the different levels of resistance that may arise in your organization is part of your role.

Maybe you find yourself in the unenviable position of wanting to change things but not having the authority to do so. Let's say you're a leader intent on implementing specific changes to boost productivity in your department. However, you need the resources that only a top-level executive can sanction. In such a case, you have to convince the person in authority of the need for these changes.

Convincing a person in authority requires you to have good influencing and negotiating skills. A good negotiator knows how to communicate their message in a way that appeals to others. You'll need to employ your political skills to present your ideas as a win-win for everyone concerned. This is very important when trying to sell your ideas for change to the senior executives in your organization.

However, selling your ideas for change to senior executives is easier said than done. This in itself could be another hurdle because senior executives may be resistant to your ideas for change. You have to know how to handle such a situation when it arises. After going through the entire process of planning, overcoming resistance, and getting approval, you may find yourself facing the biggest problem yet. Your organization may lack the *budget and manpower* to implement the kind of changes you desire. If there is no financial commitment available to support the changes, your ideas could be dead in the water.

All the above are scenarios that happen in real organizations every single day. But as a change wizard, you cannot run from these problems or wave them away with a magic wand. Fortunately, this book provides steps to become a master of change, not a victim of the many challenges you may face along the change process.

This book focuses on key practices when it comes to leading change. In the corporate or business sphere, there is a world of difference between theory and practice. Most corporate leaders and business students are adept at learning the theories of change in an organization. Unfortunately, though these theories are widely accepted, very few organizations understand how to put them into practice.

You will learn here how to lead and influence others through change. If you want to implement lasting and effective change in your organization, you need to lead from the front. You also need to bring people on board who believe in your vision for change and are most affected by that change. Use them as influencers throughout the organization.

You will also see how to avoid and manage the major saboteurs of change. Sometimes, these can be generated by you and others. Other times, they can be systemic or structural obstacles. Most organizations have a rigid cultural, political, and structural setup to guide everyone in a particular direction toward specific goals. You need to understand this organizational setup to know how to get things moving in the right direction.

You will also discover ways of dealing with resistance to change. Sometimes, people resist change because they are comfortable with the status quo and are simply afraid of losing whatever comforts they have become accustomed to. You will learn how to be firm and decisive when adopting changes that are beneficial, yet unpopular with some sections of the organization.

It is difficult to lead an organization through change without a clear roadmap and vision of the future. This book will explain how to envision the future of your team or organization after the changes have taken effect. You should have a vision that inspires your team to not just adopt the changes but maintain them in the long run.

Nothing worth doing comes easy, and change management is no exception. Depending on the scope and scale of your changes, you will face some challenges that may test your resolve. I'm going to share some tips on how to achieve change even when it seems like the odds are increasingly against you.

Finally, I will share several tools, techniques, and models that can help you carry out the change process. These tools are very practical and will enable you to start the process well so that your organization has a better chance of adopting and sticking to the changes.

But who am I, and why should you take my advice when it comes to change management and leadership?

My name is Marlene Gonzalez, and I'm the founder and president of LCG Group, LLC. I am a certified executive coach and a licensed practitioner for Insights Discovery North America. My organization provides leadership development and coaching services. I love working with organizations to inspire and transform teams and individuals to turn the most common leadership challenges into success.

With more than 30 years of corporate, business, and non-profit experience, I know what it takes to adopt and lead the kind of changes that can take a company to the next level. I care deeply about helping you achieve change in your organization. The information you're about to learn has helped to transform a wide array of institutions, ranging from governments, non-profits, and educational institutions to Fortune 500 companies.

I want to use my wealth of experience to help you understand the importance of change in today's fast-paced world. I also want to leverage my experiences to help you reach your goals. I am passionate about helping people make important changes not only in their work but also personal life. When it comes to leading change, the principles you use in your professional life are the same as those you would use to transform your personal life. I want to teach you these fundamental, life-changing steps.

Look around you. What do you see? Changes are happening everywhere — in governments, the corporate world, and even at an individual level. There is no escaping this reality. You can choose to either learn how to adapt or fight to keep things the same. This is not a time to be fearful and shrink back into your cocoon of warmth and safety. You will only be delaying the inevitable and leaving yourself vulnerable to fear and confusion. How you manage change today will determine your level of success tomorrow. I want to help you learn how to make the right change process for yourself and your organization. This will enable you to achieve your true potential.

This is more than just another change management book. There are hundreds on this topic all over the internet. This book is different because it focuses on you and your mental attitude toward change. It teaches you how to adopt the right mindset so you can embrace and execute change anytime, anywhere. As you read through each chapter, I want you to write down any ideas that come to mind. You may have an epiphany about how to adopt a change in your personal life, career, or business. Journaling is a great way to practice mindfulness and also helps you commit to taking action.

Yes, change is often terrifying for most people. But don't be scared. Be prepared. It is said that every crisis has its opportunities. Let me show you how to navigate the rough waters of change so that you will be ready to embrace the opportunities to lead change when they arise. If you're searching for information to help you lead change, be decisive and persistent even amid resistance, this book is just what you need.

THE URGENCY FOR CHANGE

H uman beings are some of the most adaptable creatures on the planet. We have always understood the importance of changing with the seasons as a means of survival. Yet, throughout history, humanity has never been forced to adopt wide-scale changes in almost every sphere of life at the same time. This is precisely what is happening in the world right now.

All over the globe, we see massive transformations within the business landscape. Some of these changes have caught many off guard, and several organizations have been forced to play catch-up. However, other changes are the result of visionary leaders who are trying to foresee the future and making urgent transitions. As these changes continue to occur at an alarming rate, leaders must be equipped to handle them quickly and decisively.

In this chapter, you will learn the need for change in today's world. As a leader, you will discover how to be agile in adopting, embracing, and leading change. You will also discover some of the challenges as well as strategies to handle these changes.

WHY IS CHANGE NECESSARY?

A leader with considerable experience in the business world understands just how quickly the marketplace can change. One minute your company is the market leader, and the next moment, you're filing for bankruptcy because a competitor swooped in and disrupted the marketplace. A good example is the story of Blockbuster and Netflix.

When Netflix launched its video-rental services in 1997, Blockbuster was the undisputed champion of the industry with over 2,800 stores across the world. Compared to Blockbuster, Netflix was a fish in a shark tank. Three years later, Reed Hastings, the Netflix cofounder and CEO, approached Blockbuster with a proposal to merge wherein Netflix would operate an online brand for the giant chain. He asked for $50 million as part of the deal. In what would later be a very costly move, the Blockbuster CEO laughed in Hastings' face and rejected the proposal. Why would a multi-billion-dollar organization make a deal with a company struggling to raise cash for operations? And who the heck would want to stream movies online, anyway?

As they say, the rest is history. Netflix went on to launch its online movie subscription service and garnered 6.3 million subscribers by 2006. Though Blockbuster eventually launched an online platform to compete with Netflix, it was too little too late. The winds of change had come, and Blockbuster had not been prepared for the transition. In 2010, as Netflix claimed 20% of the online market share, Blockbuster was filing for bankruptcy with reported losses of nearly $1 billion. Today, the little company that wanted a $50 million cash injection has a market capitalization of over $230 billion.

You've probably studied this story numerous times and drawn your own conclusions. However, one thing is clear. Change is equal to leadership now more than ever in the history of business. Just as Blockbuster failed to keep up with the times, organizations that do not change will lose their competitive edge. Companies that refuse to embrace change will fall short of customer demands and needs. Nothing changes without a good reason. As a leader, you must realize that all change serves a purpose.

Here are five reasons why change is necessary for an organization:

Rapid Technological Changes

You've probably heard that the rate of technological change and adoption is accelerating exponentially. The World Economic Forum (WEF, 2016) indicated that we have entered the fourth industrial revolution. This means that many of the technologies you use today will be replaced in a few years by something better. These changes may not be to everyone's liking because people often get attached to the status quo. The truth is that change creates uncertainty and thus scares people.

Some people are uncomfortable with rapid changes — or any kind of change at all. Look at it this way. If it weren't for technological changes like email, you would still be dictating a letter to your secretary and editing it by hand before sending it by snail mail. Imagine all the time wasted on one simple task. Embracing technological changes makes it easier to operate and manage your business and employees.

Though adopting technological changes in an organization may cause some disruptions at first, these changes can increase productivity, efficiency, and service delivery. A good example is in the area of communication. Changes in technology now enable you to communicate instantly with people around the globe. Gone are the days when you went to a bank and waited in line to withdraw money. Time is of massive value, and you no longer need to waste it. The new banking system has evolved to make our lives easier. Think about deposits, transfers, and payments, all done from your smartphone. This was impossible 20 years ago. Now, you can find anyone online and chat. You can even download or search for whatever information you need to grow your organization.

The impossible became possible: I'm/possible. You too can be a badass change agent and break old limiting beliefs.

Evolution of Customer Needs

Every company worth its salt now has an online presence, including active social media accounts to tend to its customers' needs. In today's world, customers expect their favorite brands to be reachable 24/7. Thanks to the internet, there is no such thing as regular business hours. While the physical office may be closed, an organization's virtual presence should always be felt by its customers. Customer care representatives are now always on call to answer queries and deal with all kinds of issues. For example, you can chat with customer care agents via social media at any time of the day. You can ask questions about products, make complaints, and even ask for instructions on how to use a product or service. All this is available via a company's Facebook, Twitter, or Instagram accounts.

The needs of customers are constantly changing and growing as people keep demanding better products and services. As a business leader, you should see this as a great opportunity to innovate and invest in new areas of opportunity to meet customer needs. You no longer have to guess what they want. Just pay attention to your social media accounts, and you'll get enough information to inspire your decisions.

Global Economic Changes

What comes to mind when you think of global economic changes? Most people would quickly visualize a weakening economy and its impact on their bottom line. When the global economy weakens, you may find yourself facing difficult decisions to ensure the survival of your company. You may have to reduce your workforce, slash salaries, or scale down some of your less profitable operations. You may have to move your services online as you close down some of your offices.

But what happens when global economic changes lead to positive outcomes? Is it possible for such positive changes to create problems for an organization? The answer is yes. There are instances where global economic changes may give rise to positive outcomes in an organization. However, those positive outcomes may then lead to business challenges that the organization must contend with. Let's dive deeper into this.

Positive economic changes present their own set of challenges to an organization. When the economy is booming, there is usually a rise in the demand for goods and services. Companies may have to consider expanding operations by opening new facilities and hiring more employees. Though these changes may be positive, they do present an organization with new challenges during the transition period. As a leader, understanding the need for change increases your awareness of what's happening in the global economy. You are always prepared to handle both the positive and negative outcomes of change.

Employee Training and Growth

As the business environment changes, everyone within that environment must be equipped to cope with those changes. One of the changes we're witnessing today is an increase in the number of employees demanding greater flexibility and control over their work lives. In the United States, more Americans are choosing to quit their full-time jobs and work part-time or engage in freelance work. Many young, college-educated Americans want more control over their careers and personal lives. This mass exodus from the conventional 9-to-5 workplace means that it will no longer be business as usual. Therefore, organizations should prepare their employees by training them to use new tools and learn new skills to maintain productivity. Employees should be encouraged to explore new opportunities and creative ideas in ways that serve the organization's interests.

To achieve this, there must be an analysis of the tools and training necessary for learning new skills. The organization should undertake a thorough evaluation of employees' capabilities and then provide training either in a conventional classroom setting or via online learning. Take steps to fill in any gaps that may exist between an employee's current skills and the skills needed to grow their capacity. It is also important to routinely gauge employees' performances to determine their level of potential and reward top performers. As a leader, you also need to upgrade your skills regularly through continual learning and leadership training.

Challenging the Status Quo

There are times when company leaders and employees have to question the way they are doing things. Though maintaining the status quo is the default position in the minds of many, challenging established norms can lead to great benefits. The simple act of asking "Why?" can help you come up with new ideas and innovations that improve the profitability of an organization. For example, you can explore new ways of meeting customer needs, creating better products, delivering services, or improving customer interactions. A leader who constantly challenges the status quo becomes more creative and innovative.

In most cases, existing employees may not feel the need to challenge the status quo. Fortunately, this is one area where new employees can offer a lot more value than the existing ones. Recruits usually look at the organization with a fresh pair of eyes. They can pinpoint areas of improvement that existing employees have overlooked.

Adding new people to your workforce can be a positive change, but don't let your existing employees off the hook. Encourage them to question the existing processes and systems. You want your employees to be constantly thinking of how to provide a higher quality of products and services. At the end of the day, any new idea that enables work to be done better and faster should be explored.

BENEFITS OF EMBRACING CHANGE

As the business world evolves, most of the changes will focus on digital transformation. The COVID-19 pandemic of 2020 exposed every business to scrutiny. Those who were not prepared to switch to a digital economy were caught flat-footed. While some organizations managed to ensure a somewhat seamless move toward their digital platforms, others were left behind to struggle with the new rules. Those that were strategically positioned digitally had already started minimizing face-to-face interactions by adopting digital alternatives.

Digitization is the new normal. Though we already had social media platforms, they have now become the primary way to maintain relationships and access entertainment. There is increased interest in cryptocurrencies, Non-Fungible Tokens (NFTs), and Decentralized Finance (DeFi). Online education and homeschooling are becoming more acceptable. Some governments are working on a national digital currency. Even religion has become digitized as people attend online prayer services.

On top of that, digitization is also taking over the workplace. More employees are working from home. Companies now have to provide their staff with the ability to work safely and seamlessly from remote locations. Automation and digitization provide the kind of flexibility that can help a company stay ahead of its competitors. Any organization that is *still thinking* about making these changes may end up like Blockbuster. But what are the specific benefits that come with adopting and embracing change? Here are three main benefits of embracing change:

Increase in Revenue Potential

One of the most obvious benefits of embracing digital changes is the potential increase in revenue. According to the WEF, businesses that didn't have a digital strategy in 2018 missed the opportunity to increase their revenue by

15%. By 2023, companies with a digital strategy will potentially grow their annual revenue by 43%. The report also indicated that by the year 2025, digital ecosystems could be responsible for as much as 30% of global corporate revenue. WEF projects that the rate of digital purchases could increase by 160% by 2024. As digitized health care becomes a reality, projections also show that telehealth could see a growth of 20% by 2024 (WEF, 2020).

As with every crisis, there are winners and losers. Companies that have been investing in developing strong digital systems have managed to weather the unexpected storm caused by the pandemic. Some experienced tremendous gains as others were being severely hit by the pandemic. For example, *Wexer*, a British online fitness content provider, reported a whopping 780% increase in users since the start of the pandemic. This goes to show the impact that digital transformation can have on a company that is prepared to adopt the required technological changes.

This is not to say that every business must ditch their brick-and-mortar offices and go fully online. The truth is that some companies cannot operate solely over the internet. However, the above examples prove that having digital mechanisms in place can make the difference between a successful pivot and a staggering collapse. As a leader, you must have the vision to antici-pate such kinds of technological disruptions. As the world moves deeper into the digital age, you must have a team that keeps up with these digital changes so that your organization is not caught off guard or left behind technologically.

Improvement in Efficiency

Digitizing tasks and automating processes is a good way to boost the efficiency of your business. Doing so allows your business to save time and focus resources on tasks that are of higher value to the company. Employees can work, and you can engage your teams in projects that have a greater impact on productivity and revenue growth. A digital strategy means that any disruptions will not impact your company negatively. You will be able to continue your business operations through its automated and digitized systems.

Digital transformation also boosts your ability to collaborate with remote workers. More companies are investing in collaboration software such as Slack, Trello, Asana, and Microsoft Teams. Collaboration software has been around for a couple of years, and it's a trend that has gained more attention recently due to the large number of employees working from home. The type of software you choose will depend on your priorities (collaboration or communication), budget, and size of your team.

On the other hand, some essential processes still need in-person communication. This is especially true when it comes to talent recruitment and personal development. The good news is that the time saved by automating some processes can be channeled into these essential services.

Identification of Growth Opportunities

Digitization and automation improve your ability to identify and seize opportunities for business growth. When businesses transition from analog to digital services, they make room for developing creative solutions to problems. Think of a company that stores its customer records on paper files. Every record or correspondence from customers goes into a paper-based catalog, resulting in a huge amount of data that employees have to thumb through when serving customers.

By changing its paper-based system to a digital one, the company can easily improve its document workflow and free up time for its employees. Artificial intelligence (AI) and machine learning can be used to speed up this process, removing the need for any manual intervention. Furthermore, digitization and automation will enable greater access to more data variables, enhancing efficiency and innovation.

Since employees no longer have to look through so many paper files, they can channel their time and energy to providing better customer service. They can start looking at existing problems and come up with new ideas and solutions. As a result, it becomes easier to search for growth opportunities within the industry and beyond.

THE MAJOR SHIFTS OCCURRING RIGHT NOW

The business world is transforming at a rapid rate. With so much happening so fast, it's important to find ways to leverage these changes to drive the growth of your business. Most of the changes we are experiencing at the moment have been in the pipeline for a long time. The COVID-19 pandemic has simply accelerated the timeline for the transformations we are witnessing. Though it has been difficult for most people to handle, as a collective, we have adapted quickly to survive. Many people are starting to change their perspective on things like homeschooling and remote work. When conditions change, you must find ways to adapt.

It is this same approach that business leaders must take. You need to find ways to ensure that your business adapts, pivots, and evolves with the changes that are happening. Anyone who thinks that the rate of change is going to slow down is delusional. There will be a massive acceleration of change moving forward, and you will have to anticipate the challenges that these changes will create. However, with every challenge comes an opportunity for your business to grow. All you have to do is be prepared to see and seize the potential bounty in every challenge. Here are four key areas that you need to pay attention to if you want to grow your business:

The Remote Workspace

Gone are the days when you had hundreds of employees sitting in offices, working from 9-to-5 under the watch of a hawk-eyed boss. Working from home appears to be part of the new normal. There was a time when business leaders wondered whether their employees could be productive working from home. This question is being answered right now as millions of workers now work from home while trying to maintain the same level of efficiency.

But is this a temporary interruption of service or is remote work here to stay?

Let's look at the data. According to the U.S. Bureau of Labor and Statistics, only 7% of American workers worked from home regularly before the COVID-19 pandemic. This figure was much higher in European countries such as Denmark and Sweden, where as many as 20% of employees worked remotely (*Ojala & Pyoria, 2017*). Most of these remote workers were white-collar professionals or "knowledge workers," such as executives, financial analysts, information technology managers, and accountants. A Gallup poll published before the pandemic showed that 54% of office workers were willing to quit their jobs if they found one that allowed them to work remotely. This shows that the majority of employees prefer to work outside a conventional office setting.

But what's the situation post-pandemic? Here is what the research shows us: About 64% of employees in the United States now work from home (*Society for Human Resource Management, 2020*). Will this trend continue? Though some employees say that they want to go back to their offices, others would rather keep working remotely. Another Gallup poll revealed that while 41% of workers want to go back to their workplace, 59% want to work from home. Other studies reveal that even those who want to return to the office would prefer to work from home a few days per week. It seems that most employees want some kind of flexible arrangement from their employers.

Though working from home has its benefits, it also has challenges. It's not easy to maintain a strong culture when most of your employees are working remotely. Innovation and creativity often occur when people are working together physically in the same space. Processes such as training and onboarding are more effective when they are done in person.

According to the *Vistage CEO Confidence Index Survey*, about 63% of chief executive officers (CEOs) have plans for their employees to return to work in some way after the pandemic. About half of these CEOs said that they would allow employees to choose whether to work remotely or stay in the office. Others indicated that they would implement a phased approach where some workers would return to the office while others worked from home.

It seems that the answer may lie in adopting a hybrid model. This way, the company can still reap the benefits of people coming together to achieve the organization's goals. The situation is very fluid right now, and companies will have to test different strategies to find the best model that works for them.

The Reinvention of Physical Offices

As remote work and teleworking gradually become a reality, there will be a dramatic shift in the requirements for office workspace. Research shows that organizations are taking strong measures to reconfigure their workspaces to ensure that employees feel physically safe. This is due to the new COVID-19 requirements for social distancing.

In a survey of small and medium-sized businesses (SMBs), 60% of leaders stated that they had developed a robust plan to bring employees back to work. Overall, 68% of business leaders were confident that their workers would feel safe going back to work (*Vistage Q2, 2020*). Some of the factors that CEOs are considering as they prepare their physical office spaces are employee expectations, commute times, real estate, and costs of preparation.

Less Business Travel

Before the pandemic, business executives would travel across the globe to meet with their counterparts and clients. With the restrictions on air travel during the pandemic, business travel ground to a halt as people were forced to connect digitally. We may not see the same levels of business travel return. In some ways, digital applications have shown that it isn't necessary to hop on a plane or travel long distances to interact with others. Many businesspeople — even those who considered themselves digitally challenged — have now learned how to use video conferencing software like Zoom, Skype for Business, and Adobe Connect to hold virtual meetings. Many are realizing that digital alternatives can be just as effective as face-to-face communication.

This doesn't mean that all in-person business meetings will become obsolete. There is, and always will be, a place for in-person gatherings. This is especially true for SMBs that often rely on personal connections with customers and clients. It is a major challenge that many SMB business leaders are facing right now. Sometimes, you have to physically meet and talk to a customer or business prospect. For many business leaders, facetime with clients is the most critical part of developing and maintaining a strong business relationship. This is also critical during specific stages of a sales cycle when you need to be in the same room with someone to create that human connection.

The reality is that as a business leader, you now have to find new ways of having meetings. You may have to reconsider how regularly you hold in-person meetings as you also think about how to effectively use the power of technology to create and maintain relationships.

Acceleration of Digital Transformation

Way back in 2005, the term "digital transformation" was merely a buzzword that was bandied about among tech geeks and cyber nerds. The internet infrastructure was still in its nascent stage, and few businesses were even thinking about its impact. Fast forward 16 years and it has become a concept that everyone has to deal with.

Today's technologies have allowed companies to grow and thrive in ways that were not possible nearly two decades ago. There has been rapid adoption of technology as the core driver of innovation and a solution for many business challenges. This has energized the efforts of many organizations to transition to a more digital way of doing business.

But as with all things, some organizations are far ahead of others in this digital transformation process. These early adopters are the ones who experienced less disruption during the pandemic and were able to recover and adapt much faster than the rest. Such companies are now doubling down on their efforts to transform their systems to improve performance and productivity now and in the future.

Whether your company is struggling or not right now, the truth is that you must prepare for continual changes as well as future challenges. This is the only way that your business will realize the opportunities ahead. The road to recovery is going to be long with a lot of ups and downs along the way. Some believe that it may take years before the world economy gets back on its feet. There could be unseen challenges that arise as we move ahead. Remember that you have to learn how to adapt, survive, and thrive. With this kind of mentality and resilience, you can lead your organization to new heights even amid unprecedented global changes.

STRATEGIES FOR HANDLING GLOBAL CHANGES

Now that we've covered the major changes occurring in the business world and their potential benefits, it's time to ask a key question. What does all this mean for you as a business leader? The short answer is that you need to adapt to these trends. Here are some ideas to consider:

Leverage Your Business Technology Solutions

Just because social distancing and remote work have become the norm doesn't mean your business communications have to suffer. You still need to ensure that information is passed along, meetings are held, and projects are completed on time. Technology solutions can help you improve your business outcomes and boost productivity.

One communication technology you can adopt is VoIP (Voice over Internet Protocol). This technology allows you to use the internet to make phone calls. You can set up all your office voicemails to be transferred to your email so that you can check them remotely. Videoconferencing is also an alternative to in-person meetings and can boost collaboration and lower travel costs. You can also use business messaging platforms like Microsoft Teams to stay in touch with your employees and support your teams virtually. It allows you to chat with team members, share documents, and receive instant messages via the mobile app.

Stay Optimistic

As companies around the world face financial and logistical constraints, many business leaders are finding it tough to help their employees stay positive. The leaders themselves are worried. They are afraid that if they focus too much on positivity, they may be perceived as being out of touch. Instead of raising people's spirits, their optimism may backfire. Yet these fears are unfounded because research shows that the opposite is true. It is precisely in the middle of a crisis that leaders should take active steps to infuse positivity in their employees.

Take the example of Genesis Medical Center in Davenport, Iowa. In 2017, the medical center was facing massive cost cuts and layoffs due to a drop in profitability. Staff members were being asked to take time off and reduce their working hours. In an attempt to add more positivity to the hospital, the company president decided to implement a series of positive psychology interventions in some departments. It included things like gratitude exercises, deliberate acts of kindness, and more recognition and praise from managers. Since a staggered approach was adopted, some departments were exposed to the positivity interventions before others.

When those who had not received the interventions were asked whether the hospital was going in the right direction, only 37% agreed. When the same question was put to the departments that had participated in the positivity interventions, 63% of respondents answered in the affirmative. The number of respondents who said they felt burned out reduced from 11% to 6%. More employees felt socially connected, with 85% of respondents saying they felt connected at work. This was despite the fact that many workers had lost friends due to the staff reductions.

When things aren't going well and there is a lot of uncertainty in the air, people look to their leaders to reassure and encourage them. As a business leader, you need to step up and be the face of optimism in your company when massive changes are happening. For example, if you decide to create a positive leadership workshop, you must attend every meeting to show employees that it's a priority for you. You need to help your employees feel connected by encouraging brainstorming and group discussions. Consider making positivity a part of your organizational culture rather than waiting to introduce it when there's a crisis.

Optimism is one of the most important traits you can develop as a leader. It's the ability to stay mentally resilient even when you have no idea what may happen next. Focus on your fundamentals and stay strong even as you prepare to adapt to whatever situation that may arise.

Prepare for a New Normal

A new normal may mean different things to different people. You need to examine your business processes to determine how the current changes are going to impact your company. For example, if you were purchasing raw materials or finished products from a particular supplier, you may have to find a new supply chain. If you were importing materials from overseas, you may be forced to find a local supplier. Every decision will have a cost implication, so you need to explore your options to make the best decision possible.

As you make these decisions, you should also consider future changes that may occur within your industry. What trends are you seeing right now? What are other business leaders in your industry saying or doing? Talk to both insiders and outsiders to get a good view of any future shifts that may affect you.

The reason why you should consult professionals outside your industry is that they may see something that insiders do not. A CEO may get distracted by the everyday events of doing business and end up losing track of the bigger picture. An outsider can provide a sounding board that grounds you in real leadership duties. They view things from a different perspective and can challenge some of the decisions that industry insiders have been making for years. Think of it this way: If the industry is being disrupted, then maybe you need someone who will disrupt your normal patterns of thinking.

As you consult widely, try to see any potential surprises, and find ways of adapting to them. These changes are going to affect both your business and personal life, so always consider solutions that solve problems in both areas. Keep in mind that you aren't just hedging your bets and playing defense for your business. You are also preparing yourself to grab any opportunities that may come your way.

As the world changes, we have to be ready to adapt and embrace new ways of doing business. If you're a business leader, you cannot afford to be left behind. You must lead the change from the front. You want to be ahead of your team, watching out for obstacles, and coming up with practical solutions at all times. These changes may seem overwhelming and disruptive, but they are part of a bigger and necessary shift.

It won't be all about doom and gloom. The benefits of change range from an increase in revenue and automation to better opportunities for growth. It's the decisions you make now that will determine how your business performs during and after these changes. You can choose to be strategic and learn to roll with the punches or you can leave things to chance and fight with emotions. Every great boxer will tell you that you cannot stand in the ring taking punches merely hoping to survive. You must learn how and when to sidestep, block, and counterattack.

In other words, find a balance between defense (protecting your business) and offense (grabbing opportunities). You're going to get punched at some point, so you might as well have a strategy in place for when you do take a hit. As you are about to learn, part of this strategy should be staying aware of the culture and politics within your organization.

KEY TAKEAWAYS

At a time of massive global economic shifts, organizations that do not change will lose their competitive edge and likely fail to keep up with customer expectations. Here are 5 things to do to embrace change and avoid losing out to competitors:

1. *Adopt technological changes.* Take advantage of technological changes such as artificial intelligence (AI) and automation to enhance efficiency and productivity. You can use AI to

enhance your cybersecurity and detect any unusual activity in inventory or accounting. AI can also help you learn more about your customers and their unique needs.

2. *Maintain online contact with your customers.* Leverage the power of social media to connect with customers and build brand loyalty. Make regular posts on your blog or social media accounts offering customers valuable information about products or services they are interested in. You should also have active customer care representatives who are available online to answer questions and deal with potential problems.

3. *Pay close attention to global economic changes.* Use online tools and resources to make it easier to identify market trends and consumer patterns. You can subscribe to websites such as BuzzFeed, Mashable, Reddit, and newsletters from experts in your industry. Social media apps like Facebook and Twitter also have features that show you trending content based on your online activity, location, and people you follow.

4. *Use resources to train employees and upgrade their skills.* First, assess your employees' capabilities to identify their current skills level. Then,

provide the necessary training to bridge any skills gap. This can be done in a conventional classroom setting or via online learning. By enabling employees to continually improve their skills, you will enhance productivity and effectiveness at the workplace.

5. *Learn to challenge the status quo and encourage your employees to do the same.* Show a sense of urgency when you have meetings, and invite people with a different perspective to share their thoughts. Talk to employees one-on-one and ask them questions about work-related problems and opportunities for improvement. This will encourage employees to also ask questions about some of the ways things are done in the organization.

2

DIVERSITY AND POLITICAL AWARENESS

Implementing change within an organization is never a straightforward process. There are many considerations in play, including cultural differences, internal politics, organizational structure, and personalities. In this chapter, you will learn how to be aware of all these elements and what you need to do to use this knowledge to execute changes effectively.

Executing changes in an organization requires a collaborative effort. Even if you're the final authority when it comes to decision-making, you must still know how to get others on board. You need to determine whose support is necessary to adopt the changes. Once you identify your change champions and influencers, you should figure out their motivations, personality, and responses. You should also identify the gatekeepers and those who are likely to resist changes. Take the time to understand where they are coming from and what their concerns are.

Keep in mind that people are already accustomed to working under particular systems, and some of them have big egos that may pose a challenge when adopting change. Sometimes, company politics takes center stage as individuals fight against what they perceive to be a loss of their power and influence. There are both formal and informal networks within every organization, and you should be aware of how to maneuver between them.

There are times when you have to take the lead, but there are also times when you need to delegate some leadership responsibilities and support from the rear. As you do all this, be mindful of how the content and timing of your change initiative will impact your organization.

ENHANCING CULTURAL AWARENESS AT WORK

In today's modern workplace, the workforce is a heterogeneous mix of people from diverse cultures. You may have employees from different national and racial backgrounds. You may also be dealing with clients and partners from different parts of the world. Diversity brings many benefits to an organization. People of diverse cultures will bring their unique ideas, talents, and opinions, thus ensuring a dynamic and innovative workplace.

Since a person's culture influences their thoughts, speech, and behavior, you must understand these differences to avoid conflict. When you and your employees understand and appreciate these cultural differences, it becomes easier to implement change within the organization. Having a cultural awareness means you know how to motivate and inspire every individual based on their unique background and perspective of life. Sometimes, people resist because they feel that their cultural experiences are being ignored or maligned by that change. Therefore, enhancing cultural awareness makes it easier to get people working together to achieve a collective goal. Here are some practical steps you can take to create cultural awareness in your organization:

Step 1: Establish Guidelines and Policies

You should set some rules and policies that guide your employees, especially when it comes to cultural diversity. These policies enable them to be culturally aware so that they understand what is acceptable and ethical in the workplace. These rules will make it clear how people from diverse backgrounds should relate to one another. All policies you establish in your company must be compatible with the local laws that deal with workplace discrimination. Once you have reviewed and aligned your local laws and company guidelines, make sure that everyone from the top down is aware of what discrimination is and how to be culturally sensitive.

Step 2: Celebrate Holidays and Festivals

Having a diverse workforce is a great opportunity for everyone to learn about new cultures. Every culture has its unique heritage that can often tell you a lot about a person's background and values. By asking questions and listening to your employees' stories about their heritage, you can gain a deeper understanding of their personalities. You can show them that you value diversity by wishing them well on their religious or cultural holidays. You can include their traditional holidays and festivals in the company news bulletin or email and find time to celebrate the occasion at work. This will show your employees that you recognize their cultures.

One of the best ways of engaging with a different culture is through food. You can schedule a monthly outing where employees go to a restaurant that serves cuisine from around the world. You can also ask staff members to share recipes for their favorite meals. When staff members celebrate religious or cultural holidays, bring in snacks from their culture to share with others. You can also have an "international food day" when staff members from diverse backgrounds bring a traditional dish to share.

By introducing your employees to new traditions, you can create shared experiences bridging the gap between different cultures. This will also enhance their sensitivity to cultural differences, and they may pick up a few foreign words that may be useful when communicating with other foreign colleagues and clients.

Step 3: Promote Clear Communication

Most workplace conflicts stem from poor communication and misunderstandings. When you have employees from diverse backgrounds, you are dealing with people who communicate with different verbal and non-verbal cues. For example, some cultures advocate for direct eye contact as a sign of trust. However, the same act is considered rude in other cultures. In some cultures, especially in the west, it's encouraged to be expedient and efficient when talking to your superiors at work. A manager doesn't have much time for chitchat, so employees better say what's on their mind quickly. But in other cultures, being direct with your boss is perceived as disrespectful. It is important that you learn the subtle communication nuances that are part of different cultures. You do not want to send the wrong message to those you're communicating with.

You should spend more time exploring different cultural communication styles, especially if you have a diverse workforce or clientele. This will provide you with a better context for understanding how other people's verbal and non-verbal communication cues differ from yours. This will also help you align the various communication styles to enhance efficiency and productivity.

Step 4: Learn from Different Cultures

One of the benefits of being culturally aware is that you get to learn about the different areas of the world. Let's say you've hired employees of different nationalities. You should find ways to show them that you acknowledge their diversity. You can place a large map in the common room and ask them to mark their countries of origin. This can be a great way to start conversations and learn about other cultures.

When you learn from different cultures, you also begin to think about your own. Every time you experience a behavior from someone of a different culture, ask yourself whether you also display behaviors that are unique to your culture. By examining yourself in the same light, you'll realize that the more you understand other cultures, the more you know yourself.

Step 5: Train Employees for Global Citizenship

Once you have built your employees' cultural knowledge, you can move on to formal training for global citizenship. These are classes where people learn about different cultural practices and how to work effectively in a global economy. For example, if your organization does a lot of business with clients from India, you can hire someone who has experience working in India to train your employees. This formal training should

CHANGE WIZARD | 61

cover aspects that you need to be familiar with when in a business setting. These include business etiquette, communication skills, marketing skills, and negotiation tactics.

Step 6: Enhance Your Communication Skills

If you want to execute change, you have to make sure that your message is understood loud and clear by everyone concerned. This becomes a bit more complex when you have employees from different cultures. Your communication skills will determine whether the message is received and implemented properly. If some of your employees are not native English speakers, advise your other staff members to avoid long sentences and colloquialism. They should also avoid using humor or sarcasm as these may create confusion or be interpreted the wrong way. They should also ask foreign workmates to clarify their messages and requests by email or face-to-face. These measures will keep mistakes and misunderstandings to a minimum.

Step 7: Practice Good Manners

Having good manners is a critical aspect of doing business regardless of where you are in the world. It doesn't cost you anything to use words like "please" and "thank you" in your speech. Doing this shows people that you are caring, respectful, and polite. Such etiquette in business can also open up many doors for you. Practicing good manners may sometimes feel unnecessary, especially if you often communicate a certain way. But in some countries, being informal with someone you're not used to is considered inappropriate. You should also use localized nuances of etiquette when in a foreign country.

Step 8: Pay Attention to Foreign Colleagues and Customers

You can also develop cultural awareness by simply listening to and observing the behavior of foreign workmates and customers. If you're based in a foreign country, your employees should take the time to study how the locals behave and do business and then adopt similar behavior. This means they have to learn how to listen more than they talk if they want to notice these subtle nuances.

Sometimes, when we see a foreigner acting a certain way, we're quick to label it as odd because we find it confusing, or even frustrating. This is why it's important to understand the underlying logic and values behind these actions and behaviors. Once you know the values underpinning that particular behavior, it's easier to respond rationally and avoid cultural conflict.

Step 9: Pay Attention to Time Zone Differences

Employees need to be aware of time zone differences when communicating with foreign customers. It may be business hours in your country, but your foreign customer may have already left work or even be asleep. Paying attention to the time zones will also help you know whether to greet a customer with a "Good morning" or "Good evening". You can always keep track of the different zones by using the online world clock.

Developing cultural awareness can be a major step in improving communication between diverse people and enhancing workplace unity. These are two vital ingredients for adopting changes in an organization. You need to avoid the kind of misunderstandings and miscommunications that can set back the entire change process. You also want everyone to work together synergistically to ensure that changes are executed quickly and effectively.

BUILDING YOUR POLITICAL SKILLS

Getting people with diverse personalities and viewpoints to collaborate and embrace change can be quite challenging. You have to know which buttons to push and how to wield both the carrot and the stick. You need to understand how to sell the new vision in a way that entices even the most ardent opponent. In other words, you need to be the kind of leader who has strong political skills.

If you look closely, you'll realize that politics is like a game of chess. You have different pieces with different strengths on the board. These pieces must collaborate and shift positions to survive and stand a chance of winning. A great chess player knows when to sacrifice a piece to entice and trap their opponent. Every move is made for the sake of achieving the overall strategy. Without a doubt, chess is a game of political skills.

This is where some people can get confused. We have been programmed — thanks to mainstream media — to believe that political skills are all about devious and underhanded schemes to manipulate people and defeat the "other side". This is not true. Developing political skills is very different from being political. Someone political is only interested in talking about politics and arguing about which side is right or wrong. It's well documented that talking about politics in the workplace can hurt relationships.

The truth is that leaders with political skills don't focus solely on manipulation and arguments. Political skills refer to the ability to understand people and influence them in ways that add value to personal or organizational success. Developing these skills simply means creating a wide network of connections and building trust among people. In business, strong political skills can help you foster relationships with your superiors, peers, and subordinates.

Research shows that having strong political skills is an essential trait for a transformational leader. A study published in the *Leadership & Organization Development Journal* found that political skills are an important component of transformational leadership and job satisfaction in managers. The study also showed that good political skills lead to more happiness and engagement at the workplace. Employees who are more engaged with their work showed a higher level of political skills and transformational leadership than those who were not.

Does this mean that you cannot be a leader without good political skills? No, there are many leaders out there who aren't as politically skilled. However, if you look at some of the best leaders or managers you've ever worked with, you'll notice that they all had great political skills. A leader who doesn't develop their political skills is going to struggle to reach people with their message and may lack the kind of influence to get things moving.

POLITICAL SKILLS A LEADER NEEDS

To develop good political skills at the workplace, you need to excel in four major areas: networking, sincerity, social astuteness, and interpersonal influence. A leader who has developed all the above traits will have a better chance of influencing people and getting things done for the organization. This will also positively affect their career trajectory.

Networking

Networking is your ability to access the people, information, and resources you need to identify a problem and its potential solutions. It is also the ability to get things done by leveraging the power of your social connections. Successful leaders tend to spend more time building their networks than their less successful peers. This is a result of surrounding themselves with people who can advise them and advocate on their behalf. When it comes to advocating for changes within an organization, a leader with a good network can quickly find change champions who will convey the message to as many people as possible. This also means that they can make better and faster decisions that have the support of other influential people.

Advising someone to network may sound like a cliché, and it may seem that a lot of people already do this. However, research shows that many managers struggle to develop their network, with about 60% of young millennials having trouble in social settings. As a political skill, networking can help you shape your environment and overcome any opposition to your goals. However, it requires self-confidence, a strong will, and the ability to be blunt when necessary.

How do you improve your networking skills?

You don't have to be an extrovert to be good at networking. Introverts can also develop their networks. The only difference is that introverts do their networking differently. You also need to be strategic and systematic when planning your networking. You don't have to attend every networking event as some won't be as useful as others. Meaningful networks are built over time, and you have to be patient as you engage with others and show them your value and expertise.

Sincerity

Sincerity as a political skill sounds a bit odd. Most politicians are well known for their extraordinary ability to speak and maintain contradictory positions or beliefs to please people. But outside of politics, sincerity is a major factor for good leadership. Of all the traits that good leaders possess, it is their sincerity that lays the foundation for their success and that of their organization. This is especially true when you're trying to get people to transition from the status quo and embrace something new. Your employees will want to know why the change is necessary, and you have to provide them with a genuine and honest explanation. You cannot afford to be disingenuous with the same people who you expect to help make the changes you seek. A lack of sincerity, when discovered, may lose you all the political goodwill you need to execute and maintain the change long term.

Sincerity doesn't mean you have to appease or mollycoddle people. It simply means you care about the people you're working with and that everyone involved is an important member of the team. If something goes wrong, a sincere leader will administer the necessary discipline, but they will also praise outstanding work. It means treating people the way you would want to be treated. At the end of the day, being sincere doesn't mean everyone will become your buddy and agree with your decisions. However, you're more likely to earn the trust and respect of both superiors and subordinates.

Interpersonal Influence

This is your ability to persuade others as a way of achieving particular goals and shape your environment. It is a form of social pressure that an individual exerts on others through the use of hard or soft tactics. As a leader, there are times when you have to convince people to perform a task by exerting pressure and being assertive. You may have to implement changes by making unpleasant decisions that affect others negatively.

For example, if a company has to cut costs, a manager may decide to lay off some employees to achieve their financial goals. This is never an easy thing to do for a leader. But firing people to reduce expenditure may be the only or best option available, and you have to know how to handle such a scenario. The bottom line is that you have to be prepared to take hard measures to achieve certain organizational goals. Making these kinds of tough decisions is part of your role as a leader. Sometimes, you have to adopt a hard approach when engaging with others within the organization.

However, interpersonal influence can also take a soft approach, for example, through consultations, personal appeals, or rewards. If you want your employees to adopt a more innovative way of working, you can appeal to them by promising them a reward when the changes succeed. Both of these approaches can be used to benefit the company and the employees. A leader who has developed this skill knows that the end goal is to gain the support of others to accomplish a given task.

Social Astuteness

This is the art of understanding people and reading social trends. A socially astute individual can interpret their behavior and that of others in a social situation and then use this information to respond diplomatically and effectively. Social astuteness is a critical factor in dealing with company politics and is indispensable for anyone in a leadership position. But you don't need to be in a position of leadership to practice social astuteness. Studies show that employees who are more socially astute perform better at work and have more positive interactions with others.

Of all the four attributes, it is social astuteness that has the greatest association with political skill and transformational leadership. Social astuteness involves accurately reading others' emotions, building a good reputation, and understanding and engaging in meaningful company politics. These are all skills that you need to develop if you're going to shepherd any changes within your organization.

Anyone can develop political skills. However, individuals have different personality traits, and some will be more naturally suited to political skills than others. The bottom line is that organizations should ensure that employees at least have opportunities to develop their political skills. They should also change their recruitment process to identify individuals who have the political skills necessary for management positions.

HOW TO IMPROVE YOUR POLITICAL SKILLS

It should now be clear that by developing your political skills, you can learn to become an effective leader. You can become the type of leader who is confident, trustworthy, delegates responsibilities, and knows how to inspire others to work together to achieve a shared vision. A leader with good political skills knows how to bring out the best in others as a way to empower both them and the whole organization.

But for some, this isn't an easy process. Some people are not naturally gifted with political skills and have to work harder to become effective leaders. The good news is that there are steps to hone your political skills. Here are some of the things you need to do:

Practice Mindfulness

One of the main characteristics of a good leader is that they always think before they speak. Let's say you're facing a frustrating situation at work that is threatening to spiral out of control. Your first instinct may be to get angry and start shouting at your subordinates. This may seem effective at first, but you're only making things worse in the long run. Speaking off the cuff may cost you the support of co-workers, and they may view you as someone who lacks emotional control. Take a more mindful approach and think about what you intend to say before you say it. Politics is about impulse control and weighing your words before saying anything.

Develop Strong Social Skills

The workplace is not just a business environment. It is also a social setting with people of diverse character and interests. This means that you have to learn how to read their cues and adapt accordingly. Think of a savvy politician and look at how they related to people during their social interactions. Were they standoffish and socially awkward or did they have a seemingly magical ability to relate to everyone around them?

To get a good idea of political skills in action, take some time to observe the different social situations in your workplace. As you watch people interacting, try to read their social cues and interpret the meanings behind their behavior. Observe how people relate to one another to strengthen a connection and achieve a goal. This is a good way to learn how to read people so that when you enter a social situation, you can interact with others in a meaningful way. You should also learn to identify and adapt to any changes in body language.

Professional Organizations and Networks

Have you ever attended a business event and met someone who walked around handing out their business card to everyone they met? This is not an effective strategy when it comes to networking. Politically savvy leaders understand that meaningful networks are built deliberately and over time. You have to network gradually and focus on connecting with people who can help you reach your goals and vice versa. Networking should never be one-sided. You cannot say you have a strong network if you are always on the receiving end and never reciprocate. Having political skills means understanding the need for quid pro quo and being comfortable with reciprocal relationships.

Practice Good Communication Skills

Political savviness means having the ability to communicate a message that inspires and resonates with others. When communicating with your colleagues, make sure your message is presented clearly and well understood. This applies to both one-on-one interactions as well as group meetings. How you handle yourself when you communicate says a lot about you as a leader. Leaders who have effective communication skills can convince more people and mobilize enough support to achieve their goals.

Be Transparent

Some would argue that there are times when a leader must conceal particular issues from those under them. However, this may not be a good idea at the workplace. If there is a problem at work, the leader must openly address the issue with employees. Political skills mean highlighting any problems hindering the effectiveness of the team and then getting people to solve them collectively. By concealing such issues, you may end up with a reputation as a weak and ineffective leader.

Be Assertive

Being assertive is a major aspect of strong leadership. This shouldn't be confused with aggression or arrogance. Assertiveness refers to expressing your thoughts and feelings directly and honestly while still respecting the rights of others. An assertive leader is not afraid of sharing opinions, desires, and beliefs as they interact with others. Your subordinates need to know that you're firmly in charge as you treat them with decency and respect. At the same time, you also cannot afford to be passive when communicating with your superiors. If you have a different opinion, make it known, and explain why you think so. Being assertive earns you more respect as a leader than aggression or passivity ever will.

Avoid Political Talk

Every time people start to talk about actual politics, things can get heated pretty quickly. Unlike the others mentioned above, political talk is one skill that you must *not* cultivate at the workplace. In a recent survey, more than 20% of Americans reported that they had quit their jobs due to a toxic environment, with one of the reasons highlighted being political arguments (SHRM, 2019). About 34% of the respondents claimed that their company did not allow divergent political views. Political talk should not be allowed in the workplace simply because it has the potential of forcing people to take sides. Before you know it, your workforce is split into factions and unable to collaborate to achieve the organization's goals.

NAVIGATING OFFICE POLITICS

The word "office politics" tends to have a negative connotation. It conjures up an image of a workplace where backstabbing, betrayal, and malalignment are the norm. While some may thrive in such an environment, most people would agree that this kind of toxic setting is bad for business. However, this is not the kind of office politics that we're going to explore. There is a different kind that is more benign and exists in every organization. In this type of office politics, you don't have to compromise your values and hurt others.

Whether you like it or not, you have to know how to navigate office politics if you intend to promote yourself and climb the corporate ladder. You can practice them fairly and properly to further your goals and those of your team. At the same time, you should also learn how to identify the bad type of office politics that causes some to benefit as the rest suffer.

But why does politics exist in the workplace? Why can't we just perform our office duties and leave politics aside? The reality is that the workplace is filled with human beings, and humans tend to have ambitions, desires, emotions, and insecurities. Everyone who goes to work has their own professional goals, and they will try to use the existing system within the organization to achieve personal success. The problem is that those goals are not always aligned and since people have different personalities, there's bound to be some conflict in the workplace. Office politics emerge when there is a clash between different personalities and ideas on how to get things done.

Additionally, we have workplace hierarchies where some people have more influence and make decisions that affect the lives of everyone else. This is the natural order of things and there is no getting around it. Since individuals become concerned when decisions are being made about their lives, there is always a desire to influence such decisions. Whereas some people are transparent about how they intend to do this, others resort to underhanded tricks to manipulate decision-makers.

Finally, there's the problem of limited resources. An organization may not have enough resources to satisfy every department or project team. As a result, some individuals or groups may compete against others to get their needs satisfied. Unfortunately, this can often be at the expense of the collective good.

TIPS FOR SURVIVING OFFICE POLITICS

The first thing you must do to ensure positive office politics in your organization is to accept its inevitability. The nature of the politics may change as employees come into and leave the company over time, but it will always be there. Once you've come to terms with this, you need to create strategies that help you identify and understand office politics. Here are seven ways to do this:

Evaluate Your Organizational Chart

You are probably very familiar with the formal structure of your organization. However, office politics tend to bypass this structure and often follow a different path. Instead of observing the formal structure with its ranks and job titles, pay attention to where the informal power lies in your organization. Who is the real brain behind the operations? Who is the most respected? Who has the most influence over others? As you ask yourself these questions, you may be surprised to learn that the answers don't fit the formal organizational chart.

Understand the Informal Network

After you have identified where the influence and power truly lie, you should explore the people's interactions within the organization to understand the informal networks. You need to be discreet and respectful as you do this so as not to arouse suspicion. Observe people closely and identify which individuals or groups are close friends and those who don't get along. Keep an eye out for cliques as well as out-groups. Find out if these connections are based on respect, friendship, or romance. As you do all this, identify how power and influence flow between these groups and individuals.

Create Your Personal Network

Once you have understood the existing informal networks, you should begin to create your social connections. Go beyond your usual team members and build connections across the formal hierarchy. Think about adding colleagues, managers, and even executives to your new social network. This may seem daunting, especially if you intend to connect to individuals high up the corporate ladder. But the secret is to be genuine in wanting to know them instead of resorting to mindless flattery.

It's also advisable to maintain camaraderie with everyone instead of aligning yourself with only one group. Politics is a fluid game, and the group that holds more power and influence today may be usurped by another tomorrow. It's best not to keep all your eggs in one basket.

Develop Strong Interpersonal Skills

There can be no politics without people. Therefore, you should focus on developing your people skills so that you can build and maintain your network. A good way to do this is by cultivating emotional intelligence. By learning to reflect and regulate your own emotions, you can gain a deeper understanding of yourself and others. You will be able to identify and understand the emotions of people around you as well as their preferences and aversions. By enhancing your emotional intelligence, you also become a better listener — and everyone loves a good listener!

Leverage your Network

You can use your workplace network to build your professional profile. By informing them of your achievements, you can get their help to connect to opportunities that may enhance your career. Just make sure that you don't pester people in your network to do you favors. Always keep your organization's goals in mind even as you try to promote yourself. You can also ask your network to give you feedback on your work. This is a great way to improve your accountability and show others that you value their opinion.

Have the Nerve but Don't Be Naïve

There are always people in the office who play dirty politics, for example, the manipulators and gossips. Most people choose to stay away from such people. However, you should take a braver approach. Instead of avoiding them, try to understand them and their goals. Be polite without being naïve enough to trust them. You don't want them to take your words and twist them to make you look bad. However, if you understand why they do what they do, you can avoid their negative office politicking. In case they try to bring you down, you'll know how to neutralize their impact.

Defuse Negative Politics

Negative office politics tend to spread when people choose to join in the fray. To defuse this negativity, don't add fuel to the fire. Don't pass malicious rumors and always check the credibility of the information. Be careful about confidential information you reveal to others and stay professional at all times. When others split themselves into factions, refuse to take sides, or get drawn into arguments. The best approach is always to consider the organizational viewpoint rather than a self-seeking one.

KEY TAKEAWAYS

Here are the key points from this chapter:

1. *An important step when implementing change is to understand the organizational culture and recognize cultural differences.* Celebrate cultural diversity by introducing a day when employees share their traditional foods or recipes. Employees can also visit an ethnic restaurant at least once a month to learn about different cultures.

2. *Social astuteness is a crucial political skill to develop.* You develop this skill by maintaining high self-awareness and working on your emotional intelligence. Pay attention to the emotions and body language of others when you speak to them. This will give you cues of whether they are responding positively to you.

3. *Focus on developing transparency and clear communication skills.* Be open about why the change is necessary and explain to all concerned exactly how the organization stands to benefit.

4. *One of the causes of office politics is personality differences.* Research different personality types to understand their motivations, strengths, and weaknesses. Use this information when

interacting with co-workers to understand their personality traits. Examine how they think and express themselves but in a non-judgmental way. You should also research effective communication to help develop verbal and non-verbal skills. Then, depending on the audience and situation, use a communication style that allows you to connect to them.

5. *To harness the power of office politics, observe the informal network around the office and identify people that share your goals.* Get to know them inside and outside of work. As you form these strong alliances, leverage this network to gather support for the changes you want to make.

In the next chapter, you will learn the importance of challenging the status quo to bring about change.

3

CHALLENGING THE STATUS QUO

I t is said that human beings are creatures of habit. Our ancestors formed habits because they realized that it was evolutionarily beneficial. By doing the same thing the same way every single time, you conserve mental energy and develop efficiency. When you form a routine, you develop a sense of familiarity, and familiarity generates positive feelings. Your brain produces endorphins and you gradually become addicted to that habit. It's your brain's way of telling you that you're on the right track. Therefore, it makes sense that you wouldn't want to challenge any of your normal routines.

But what if your habits are doing more damage than you think? Familiarity breeds contempt, and you may inevitably feel stifled and trapped by your familiar routines. Refusing to change the way you do things can lead to stagnation, lack of development, and a feeling of helplessness. In this chapter, you will learn why it's important to actively question the way things are done in your organization. You will also discover some reasons why leaders fear challenging the status quo as well as steps you can take to be a catalyst for change.

IMPORTANCE OF QUESTIONING THE STATUS QUO

The formation of habits is of great benefit to humans. Habits, rituals, and routines make us feel whole. There would never have been any progress in human evolution if we didn't form habits. Our routines ground us and help us develop essential skills that define who we are and how we contribute to society. Habits can help you become focused and disciplined enough to master a skill. Without agreeing on a specific pattern of doing things, our world would be filled with chaos and confusion.

But does that mean you should keep doing things the same way forever? No. Though maintaining your habits is beneficial to some extent, it's also important to question the status quo and challenge the existing paradigm.

One benefit of questioning the status quo is it helps avoid complacency. Think of how many times you've heard a leader say, "That's just the way we do things around here." Sometimes, you hear someone say, "We're happy with the way things are." This is a common mindset in many companies. There is a tendency to maintain the status quo as a way to avoid the risks that come with change. The problem with this kind of thinking is that it lulls you into a sense of false confidence. It leaves you at the mercy of companies that are willing to embrace change to beat their rivals.

It makes sense why a company would resist change, especially if it's profitable and has a decent share of the market. The problem is that something always comes along to trigger a change. This is a historical fact, and history has a nasty habit of repeating itself. If you've been resting on your laurels too long, the change may flip your business upside down. Your desire for familiarity and safety may leave you exposed and make it difficult for your company to stay competitive in the future.

Many companies have fallen into the status quo trap. Just ask Blackberry. Back in 2008, the Blackberry mobile phone was so popular that it was referred to as "Crackberry". At its peak, it had a market share of 20% and every business professional had one. The company was so confident in its product that it ignored the new technological advancements coming into the market. While every other smartphone maker was banking on touchscreen phones, Blackberry refused to change with the times and retained its real keyboard. This turned out to be a monumental mistake. Today, Blackberry has a market share of virtually 0% (Statista, 2020). The company has now shifted away from smartphones to software and services.

Another benefit of challenging the status quo is it keeps your company moving forward. It is one thing to avoid complacency but taking advantage of an opportunity is a whole different ball game. Questioning the status quo allows you not just to assess the benefits of making a change but also the risks of doing nothing. This is a lesson that Kodak learned the hard way.

Founded in 1888, Kodak was the largest distributor of photographic film in the world for over 100 years. At its peak, it had an 80% share of the global film and photography industry. When the digital camera was invented in 1975, the executives at Kodak dismissed the idea as unprofitable. They claimed that people would always prefer the touch and feel of a printed photograph over a digital image. They decided to stick with selling film and photographic paper.

A few years later, companies like Japan's Fuji Films were dominating the digital camera market. By the time Kodak decided to join the party, it was too late. The market had shifted from print to digital technology. Kodak tried to keep up with its rivals but failed. In 2011, the company filed for bankruptcy with the stock price of the former blue-chip company hitting an all-time low of 78 cents.

The worst thing about this story is that the man who invented the digital camera was a Kodak engineer! For years, the company had been investing money into developing new technologies. But since it was too focused on print photography, it failed to maximize the opportunity to enter the digital market. It was not just complacency that killed the company. It was the refusal of Kodak executives to move forward with speed to take advantage of new technologies.

You may be thinking that the above examples only relate to technology companies. Maybe you think that some industries cannot be influenced by technological shifts. But the truth is that every sector of the economy is now affected in some way by technology. Let's face it. We no longer live in a world of hunter-gatherers traversing the savannah seeking food, shelter, and safety. We live in a world where new information is being generated at an astronomical rate. With huge advancements in technology, we are being forced to discard a lot of the ideas we thought were true just a few years ago. Every facet of society is changing quickly, and it's easy to get left behind as an organization. You have to keep re-evaluating your systems and question some of the processes you're using at the workplace.

Status quo is a mindset. It is a mindset of complacency, fear, and risk aversion. But it is a dangerous way to run an organization, especially if you intend to improve and grow your business. Just because you have a particular system that works for you doesn't mean you shouldn't question it. And just because you've been using it for a long time doesn't mean it still works.

Questioning the status quo should become the norm rather than the exception in organizations that intend to succeed in the future. If you're leading an organization, you should be at the forefront of shaking things up. You should be encouraging your team to challenge the status quo regularly. If you do this, you will challenge your team to be continually creative, creating a culture that embraces positive change.

WHY LEADERS FEAR CHALLENGING STATUS QUO

Every organization has a specific way of doing things. It doesn't matter whether it's a family, a community, a private corporation, or a government institution. Every time a group of people come together to forge a bond to achieve a long-term goal, they end up creating habits and routines. Once these habits become the norm, it becomes difficult for anyone within the group to even perceive and question them.

But sometimes a person within the group begins to feel the need for change. They become dissatisfied with the way things are and start to question the status quo. They begin to ask and investigate whether things can be done differently. If this individual is low in the organization's hierarchy, their ideas may be easily ignored. This is especially true if the group leader doesn't embrace the idea of change. However, if a leader in the organization is the change agent, they have room to be proactive in driving and championing change.

A leader who is a change agent can assess and question the existing practices within the organization. They may discover that these practices are not generating as much value as they should or are not as beneficial as they used to be. In such a case, the change agent can seek and propose improvements to the current paradigm. They can challenge the prevailing convention and advocate for new perspectives, but they cannot do it alone. They need to find others in the organization who are willing to initiate and support the change. This is a vital step in the change process because individuals and teams can be effective catalysts in implementing change.

But sometimes a leader can shy away from challenging the status quo in the first place. In a survey by *Harvard Business Review*, over 1,000 employees across America were asked how often they have seen their senior leaders question the status quo. About 42% of respondents said that their leaders never or rarely challenged the norms. Only 3% said their leaders always did, while the rest stated that challenging the status quo happened sometimes or fairly often.

This shows that though leaders may talk and get excited about change management, they often fail to follow through on these transformative ideas. Sometimes, the front-line leaders want to implement change but the senior executives in the boardroom fail to provide the required support. As a result, leaders often refuse to go against the grain despite the benefits of adopting change. Here are five reasons why leaders often fear challenging the norm:

Fear of Accountability

A leader may be afraid of challenging the status quo because they are not willing to be held accountable. Carrying the burden of responsibility and account-ability is not an easy thing. It takes real work to reach out to others and ask for ideas on how to execute the change. You have to step out of your comfort zone and put yourself out there as a change champion. This can be scary for most leaders because once they become the figurehead of the change, the buck stops with them.

When you are tasked with making improvements in your organization, you know that senior leaders are going to demand positive results. While some people thrive on such challenges, others fear being held accountable for their actions. There are a lot of things that instill fear in the workplace, such as uncertainty, job security, and professional demands. However, leaders who fear accountability do so for two main reasons. Either they don't trust senior executives who are overseeing their work, or they are afraid of being held responsible for their performance.

If the person tasked with leading the change is a consis-tent underperformer, they will live in constant fear of accountability. Such an individual may believe that their performance is, to some degree, beyond their control so they resist taking responsibility for their failures or successes. They may blame others when things go wrong and make all kinds of excuses to deflect attention from their actions or lack thereof. A leader who fears accountability does not believe they have the power to succeed in change management. Thus, they prefer to live in fear rather than be held accountable for their failure.

Fear of Taking Risks

Making a change is risky. You have to deal with uncertainty and the probability that your efforts may not succeed. This can be overwhelming when you are the one who has to lead the change and take responsibility for it. You must be ready to put your reputation on the line, and some leaders aren't willing to do that. This fear is heightened if senior management isn't doing anything to support the one taking the risk.

However, a leader who wants to see real change must be prepared to face risks. Everybody recognizes the successful career of basketball legend Michael Jordan. He is on record saying that the main reason for his success was never being afraid to miss a shot or lose a game. He kept taking risks even after failing in previous games. Leaders who embrace risks and uncertainty will be the ones who lead their organizations to greater heights of success.

This is going to be more evident as we begin to unravel this "new normal". Nobody knows what to expect, and there is a lot of tension in the air. Some leaders are taking a wait-and-see approach, crossing their fingers that things will get better somehow. Unfortunately, this kind of mentality puts an organization at greater risk of stagnation, complacency, and predictability. Playing it safe and refusing to take risks are the worst things you can do in a business environment that is transforming rapidly and becoming increasingly competitive.

You have to embrace the risk that comes with living in uncertain times and learn how to expect the unexpected. You need to build a workplace environment where employees perform at a high level and collaborate under pressure. You and your team should learn how to adapt to whatever changes may occur in the market to stay ahead of your business rivals. So what if you fail? See it as just another stepping stone to success. This is the essence of a successful leader — to see failure as a learning opportunity rather than as a crippling obstacle.

Ignorance

Sometimes, a leader just doesn't know what to do to get things moving. This may seem surprising because we all want to believe that leaders are more informed than their followers. It is expected that if you're a leader, then you must always have an idea of how to solve a problem. But this is not always the case.

A leader may lack the entrepreneurial mindset required to bring people together and incentivize them to find creative solutions. This is not as easy as it sounds because the majority of people aren't taught how to develop an entrepreneurial mindset. Entrepreneurs focus on action, learning, growth, and achieving goals. They trust their instincts and aren't afraid of taking risks or failing. A leader who doesn't have this mentality will not want to challenge the status quo.

A leader may also be ignorant of how to align the existing expertise in their team in an optimal way to implement change. To get people to work together effectively, you need to understand everyone's strengths and how to bring out the best in all. If you don't know how to do this, you may end up with different teams working at cross-purposes.

It's also possible that a leader could be ignorant of how to effectively break down silos. Silos are groups of people who work in the same organization but behave as if they are independent of each other. For example, you may have departments that rarely communicate with each other, yet they are expected to work cohesively to achieve organizational goals. The groups have been working as separate entities for so long that it hinders the overall business objectives. A failure to break down silos can lead to a waste of resources, a lack of synergy, and an inability to learn from one another.

A lack of expertise in operationalizing change could also be a problem. Change management usually begins by having an overview of what needs to be done. To operationalize the change, you need to break down the overall strategy into programs, processes, and events. A leader who doesn't know how to do this properly will find it difficult to get the ball rolling. As a result, team members won't have the tools needed to weave the changes into the existing systems and processes. Leading change requires a fluid mindset that is aware of potential setbacks and challenges. If a leader doesn't understand how to pivot when faced with an obstacle, they may get stuck using the wrong strategy.

Lack of Organizational Readiness

Every organization has corporate values that everyone is expected to abide by. These are designed to maintain balance and ensure efficiency and productivity from leadership and employees. However, there are times when corporate values do not encourage challenging the status quo. Therefore, a leader may not be as enthu-siastic to question the existing systems because they fear going against the organization's values. Challenging the status quo would be akin to cutting off your nose.

It is also possible that the corporate values do encourage people to challenge the norm, but nobody stands by them. Leaders and their subordinates may not be consistent in working according to these values. The organization cannot experience transformation because the leader isn't actively questioning the way things are done. Instead of being inspired to do whatever it takes to ensure the organization succeeds, they go along with everything and just do as they are told. In both these cases, the leader is not prepared to challenge the norm or much less lead any kind of transformational change.

Lack of Evolution as a Leader

If you've been a leader for a long time, you have probably faced all kinds of situations throughout your career. You understand how the business environment works and how to solve the different challenges that arise in your organization. This level of experience is a huge advantage for a leader.

However, what may be a superpower can sometimes be your greatest weakness. As a senior leader working in the same organization for decades, you've formed blind spots because you've been doing things the same way for so long. You probably stopped evolving as a leader years ago and now rely on past experience to get by. But the marketplace and workplace aren't stagnant — they are constantly changing. This poses a problem to a leader who is still stuck in their old ways. They haven't evolved with the times and therefore cannot even see the changes happening, much less embrace them.

The truth is that when you challenge the status quo, you have to commit to challenging it. A lot of people talk about making changes but very few people want to challenge the status quo. As a leader, you have people who are constantly watching and gauging your leadership skills and values. A leader who adopts a fear-based mindset stifles creativity and innovation and encourages employees to be passive. Your inability to face your fears may end up costing your organization a lot of time and money while your rivals move on to greater success.

HOW TO CHALLENGE THE STATUS QUO

Challenging the status quo is rarely met with shouts of joy and pats on the back. The reaction is usually resistance, irritation, and dismissive responses designed to shut you down. Most people accustomed to doing things a particular way don't appreciate anyone rocking the boat. The workplace is no different.

Think about your current workplace. What kind of changes would you want to see right now? Maybe you've been mulling over this and have already identified a solution to a problem that's been bothering you. Maybe you desire to see more creativity or personal growth among staff members. You could be thinking on a much bigger level, for example, wanting your company to create new products or find new clients.

You probably have myriad ideas on what you would like your company to do differently. However, this doesn't mean you should storm into your workplace and begin pointing out all the things you don't like. This is unlikely to work, and you'll only end up generating resentment and resistance. It's a daunting prospect for most people to speak up and challenge the way things are done. Most people don't have the boldness to do it, and those who do are often on the receiving end of the wrath of everyone else. Fortunately, there are simple and effective ways of challenging the status quo. Here are eight steps you can take to tactfully shake things up in your workplace:

Step 1: Learn to Ask the Right Questions

In software engineering, there's a maxim that says, "garbage in, garbage out." What this means is that if you put in the wrong information, you'll receive the wrong output. This applies to interpersonal communications as well. If you ask the wrong question, you'll get the wrong answer.

One of the best questions you can ask when trying to come up with new ideas is "why". When you ask yourself this question every time you're doing an activity, you instinctively begin to think of ways to change or improve things. Once you've done this with yourself, go ahead and ask others the same question. Try to gain a better understanding of why some systems exist and whether they are being used optimally.

By asking as many people as you can, you may discover that there are good reasons why things are done that way. On the other hand, you may learn that there's no clear reason why people do things a particular way. It may be that the organization has been using that system for so long and nobody has ever thought of changing it. If you don't get a satisfactory answer the first few times, keep asking.

When you're asking your colleagues these questions, give them time to respond. Ask them open-ended questions that allow them to elaborate their thoughts rather than closed questions that require a "yes" or "no" answer. Don't forget that you're having a conversation, not conducting an interrogation. You can also use funnel questions where you start with general questions and then home in on specific points. For example,

"Do you use this filing system regularly?", "How often do you use it?", "Do you find it easy to work with?", "Has anyone else ever complained about it?", and "What is it about this system that you would change?". Using this technique helps the other person recall their experiences with the system and focus on useful details. This is more effective than if you had asked point-blank, "What don't you like about this system?".

If you suspect that an employee is afraid of talking openly, use probing questions to draw out more information from them. For example, "What exactly do you mean when you say this system is inefficient?". As they answer your questions, listen carefully to their responses as they may lead to questions or solutions that you never considered.

Step 2: Prioritize Your Ideas

If you've been contemplating potential changes within your organization, you probably have a list of ideas and solutions you would like to see implemented. You may be excited about change and want to share your passion with others around you. However, you cannot expect people to accept an avalanche of ideas within a short period. If you overwhelm them with all your bright ideas, people may tune out and dismiss you. Your good ideas are also likely to get lost amid the not-so-good ones. To ensure success when pitching ideas, select the relevant ones that are likely to be accepted. Spend some time reflecting on the ideas that are most likely to succeed and prioritize them.

Step 3: Recruit Allies

Depending on your work environment, advocating for change can be compared to going to war. You are trying to challenge systems and attitudes that have been around for a long time. But there are also others in the organization that live to protect the status quo so it's inevitable that you're going to face a lot of resistance. This means you'll need an army of your own. The more entrenched the status quo, the bigger and stronger your allies need to be.

You're not the only person in your workplace who has ideas about making changes. Find these people and gather them together as allies. By encouraging multiple perspectives on the changes needed, you will enhance creativity and inspire others to speak up. Plant the seeds of change in people's minds and ask them to share their ideas. Your allies will have your back in case there is resistance, especially if the opposition is going behind your back. Keep in mind that allies are people you're working with to bring about positive changes, so don't use their support to engage in negative office politics.

But where can you get potential allies? Allies could be your team members, experienced colleagues, your boss, senior management, support staff, executive assistants, and even clients. Building an alliance can take time, so make sure that you form high-quality connections that will help you throughout the change management process.

You should nurture your allies and support them when they need help. Ask them if they need a hand with something and keep the communication channels open. Be realistic about your demands and avoid asking for too much too soon. And if one or some of your allies refuse a request, don't take it personally. Your relationship and collaboration should be more valuable than your ego, so don't retaliate or burn bridges. They may say "no" today, and yet be available to support you tomorrow.

Step 4: Work on Your Pitch

Most people fear change because they don't know what the outcome may be. It is a touchy topic for some people who have developed a comfort zone that's conducive to their work. Therefore, you should recognize the need for tact and sensitivity. You may think you're being firm with your pitch but you're coming across as antagonistic. If you try to use force, people may shut down and reject your ideas even before you can sell them properly.

Be considerate of other people's views when pitching your ideas about change. Maybe the organization underwent a change in the past that ended up hurting employees. That may make some people simply be cautious when they hear about another change. People deal with negative experiences differently, so you need to be sensitive to everyone's emotions. Listen to what people are saying and explain to them clearly what the risks and benefits are.

Ideally, your pitch should be short and direct so that you have enough time to get feedback. Think of it as an elevator pitch when you have just a few minutes to convince the other person to collaborate with you. This means you have to spend time crafting your idea and finding the best way to communicate it. You should also pick the right time to present your ideas to people. Don't rush to sell your idea right after the inspiration hits you. You should also avoid pitching your thoughts when you're having a bad day or when the other person is stressed.

Step 5: Stay Calm and Patient

After you've given it everything you've got, you may still end up with a string of rejections as people refuse to support your ideas. Success is never guaranteed, so don't let failure and obstacles get to you. Avoid falling into a negative spiral of anger and stress. Sometimes, good ideas take time to marinate in people's minds before they are ready to be accepted. The important thing is to learn from the experience of being a change agent and focus on staying positive.

Stay calm and take time to reflect on what you've learned. Though experience is not the only way to learn, it is often the most impactful way of gaining information. You can observe others, read a book, or research online, but all the theories in the world won't transform anything until you try things out for yourself.

Step 6: Seek the Perspective of Others

Change management is not a one-man job. You need to have a team that supports and helps you come up with the best ideas possible. Therefore, you should consult as widely as possible to gather opinions of relevant stakeholders. Talk to the people on the front line, the mid-level employees, and senior executives. Some will agree with you while others may not. Some may challenge you to refine your ideas. The changes you're seeking will affect a lot of people in the organization, so consider the perspectives of others.

Step 7: Ask More Questions

We already know the importance of asking the right questions when contemplating change. Asking "why" questions help you generate ideas on what kind of changes to implement and how to go about it. However, you need to keep asking more questions throughout the process to ensure that you cover all your bases and incorporate stakeholders' opinions. You should ask yourself questions as well as others who are willing to share their perspective.

Some of the questions to ask include:

- Is there something that needs to be challenged, fixed, or improved?
- Why isn't it working?
- What can we do to fix it?
- Do you see any opportunities for improvement?
- What are the risks of making changes?
- What are the risks of doing nothing?
- What can I learn?

After you've challenged the status quo, ask yourself the following questions:

- What have I learned?

- What unexpected responses did I receive from others?
- What went wrong/right?
- Could I have done anything better?

A leader who is intent on challenging the status quo by asking questions must be prepared to receive uncomfortable answers. Have an open mind to enable you to learn and hopefully grow from the process. You also need an open heart because it makes it easier to connect with people around you. This will motivate and encourage others to work with you to adopt the change. It's also important to have an open will so that you are prepared to make risky and bold moves.

Step 8: Explore All Avenues

If you're committed to challenging the status quo, you should be prepared to explore all available avenues to implement the change. Some of the things could be risky and make you unpopular among co-workers. Some of the steps you take may force you to swallow your ego.

For example, you may have to define the status quo provocatively by making a list of how the current way of doing things is hurting the company. Some people won't like it when you share this list. The important thing is to let everyone know the cost of maintaining the status quo. Once the list is out, go out of your way to ensure that people feel safe to challenge the status quo. As a leader, show them how you will empower them and demolish the barriers to questioning the status quo.

You may have to recruit those opposed to change and convince them that it will benefit them as well. These may be people with whom you have personal issues, and you have to set your ego aside to get them on board. This is especially important if they are in a position of authority.

Another avenue you may explore is promoting people who have the habit of challenging the status quo. Some may be immature loudmouths who speak their minds a bit too openly. However, it may be easier to teach such an individual how to be a mature leader compared to trying to get a die-hard bureaucrat to embrace change. Some people work so long in an organization that they aren't interested in changing anything. You're better off working with anyone who can help you build a culture of challenging the status quo.

KEY TAKEAWAYS

Here are five action steps from this chapter:

1. *One of the reasons why a leader may fear challenging the status quo is ignorance.* For example, you may lack knowledge of how to align the expertise in your teams to implement change effectively. Get to know your team as individuals. Spend time talking to them to assess their strengths and weaknesses. Ask their colleagues and supervisors about their work patterns and behavior. You can also provide a small project to test their skills and mindset.

2. *A leader needs to evolve throughout their career and not become attached to the status quo.* One way to do this is by combining your past experiences with continual learning. Do your research and interact with people who challenge your existing beliefs. You should also consider finding a mentor to offer guidance. Try to focus on other things outside of work to broaden your perspective.

3. *As you challenge the status quo and seek change, learn to prioritize your ideas.* Don't overwhelm people with too many ideas, some of which may not be as good as others. Before pitching them, create a list of relevant ideas and evaluate their effectiveness. Ask yourself how each idea will bring change and whether it's practical, efficient, and timely. Create a shortlist of the

ones that are likely to be accepted and rank them accordingly. Pick the best one to pitch to your organization.

4. *When challenging the status quo, consult as many potential allies and stakeholders as possible.* Listen to the opinions of front-line and mid-level employees as well as senior executives. Keep an open mind, especially when challenged as this may help you to refine your ideas.

5. *Stakeholders may reject change.* If so, stay calm and positive. Don't fall into a spiral of anger and stress. Meditate on your idea and how to repackage it for greater acceptance. Consult a trusted mentor even if it's someone outside the organization as they may give you some valuable tips. People don't like surprise changes or being rushed, so give people time to reflect on your idea before trying again.

Change doesn't happen overnight. There is a process that you need to follow to prepare for it. In the next chapter, you will learn how to design an effective change process.

DESIGNING THE CHANGE PROCESS

The change process requires a high level of preparation to ensure success. This should be done on multiple levels. In most organizations, there is emphasis on preparing the systems and structures to handle the coming changes. However, your preparation needs to go beyond the normal fixation on the nut-and-bolts of the organization. You must also consider the mental attitudes that exist and how to make them compatible with the changes you're aspiring to.

Part of your preparation must involve asking yourself questions about the type of change you want to adopt in your organization. Of course, this will depend on the reasons for the change and its scope. Remember that the change process doesn't end with the completion of the project. There will still be some work to be done after that.

As you can see, there's a lot that goes into planning and executing a change process. In this chapter, you will learn how to design an effective change initiative. You will learn the steps involved in change management as well as the principles that guide it.

UNDERSTANDING THE CHANGE PROCESS

Successful organizations must evolve quickly to stay competitive and get a winning edge over their competitors. Businesses must adapt to tackle the many challenges that dot the landscape — technological changes, new competition, economic trends, and changes in regulations. To achieve this, you need to create the right mechanisms, proactively deal with market pressures, and respond to the changing needs of consumers. With this holistic approach and visionary leadership, an organization can effectively handle the challenges of the change management process.

However, moving the change process from start to finish is not as simple. Research shows that about 50% of change initiatives are unsuccessful, with 16% generating mixed results. This implies that leaders need to learn how to plan, coordinate and implement change.

But what is change management, and how should you prepare for it?

Change management refers to *the process of leading organizational change from conception, through implementation, and finally to resolution.* Organizational change may be in the form of transforming company culture, corporate hierarchy, underlying infrastructure, or internal processes.

Since the change process is future-driven, it needs to include strategies that help realize the futuristic goals of the organization. However, there are particular considerations you need to make. The most crucial factor is organizational readiness. Is your organization prepared for the changes you want to adopt? You should evaluate the level of organizational preparedness to identify any potential hiccups.

Factors that impact organizational readiness are the internal structures and systems of the organization. When assessing the existing structures, systems, and processes, you have to ask yourself one question, "Can they manage the change effectively as they are?".

You may have to reorganize some systems and structures to ensure a smoother transition process. Senior management plays a major role in doing this. As you make the necessary adjustments, understand that there is no singular approach on how to implement change. A strategy that works for one organization may not work for another. You have to evaluate and determine what works best for your organization.

You also have to consider the thoughts and emotions of people in the organization. People are the most important resource in an organization and play a key role in the change management process. As stakeholders, getting them on board will determine the growth and success of your organization. Some people may not look kindly upon change while others will support you wholeheartedly. Encourage everyone concerned to express themselves freely without fear. This can also help you know how people are likely to react to the changes.

TYPES OF ORGANIZATIONAL CHANGES

There are three types of organizational changes: adaptive, transformative, and fundamental.

Adaptive changes refer to tiny, gradual, and iterative adjustments made by an organization to improve its processes, strategies, and products over time. This is also known as developmental change. In general, this is the easiest type of change to execute because everyone can identify the need for it. It is usually a quick change that's implemented to mitigate a challenge. Therefore, though a change management plan is ideal, it may not be necessary. For example, you could recruit a new employee who is an expert in digital technologies. You could also implement a work-from-home policy for non-essential staff members or those who can execute their functions remotely.

Transformational changes refer to bigger changes that have a wider scope and signify a sudden or monumental shift from the status quo. Transformational changes must have a clear goal and a change management plan to address how the organization will transition. For example, a business may launch a new product or establish a division overseas. Improvements in operations, systems, and infrastructure also fall into this category.

Fundamental changes are large-scale shifts that affect the entire organization. Examples include leadership changes, organizational restructuring, and mergers and acquisitions. Fundamental changes may take years to implement and are often unpredictable. For this reason, a change management plan is essential to ensuring a positive outcome.

STEPS IN THE CHANGE MANAGEMENT PROCESS

The change process generally has a set of conditions that signify a starting point and a functional endpoint. There are a lot of dynamic activities that happen between these two points as the entire process unfolds in phases. Here are the five key steps in change management:

Step 1: Prepare for the Change

Any organization that wants to successfully implement change must be ready for it. A key part of change management is understanding your organization's culture — its strengths and weaknesses. Learn how your employees work and communicate with each other. You also need to know what they are good at, their preferences, and dislikes. This information can help you to prepare a good change program.

Let's say you want to implement a change in the way that project teams collaborate and communicate. The teams don't seem to work together as effectively as they should, and it's been affecting productivity. You do a bit of digging and discover that quite a number of your staff members enjoy playing video games. You could decide to organize a small video game tournament to help improve connections between the project teams.

Think of it as a team-building activity that makes it easier to adopt the change the organization needs.

Cultural preparation also involves clear communication of the change management plan. Some organizations fail to do this because they assume that sending an email announcement is enough. You need to explain to employees why the change is necessary. They can only embrace the transformation if you take the time to outline the reasons and benefits of the change. It is important to help them understand the need for change so that you can gain an initial buy-in. Clearly describe to them the various challenges that the organization is facing, or will face in the future, if the status quo is maintained.

The communication should also open up a discussion so that employees can ask questions and raise concerns. You may have to create a forum where this kind of dialog can occur. For example, you can announce the change at a general meeting when everyone gets together. After that, hold smaller meetings with individuals or teams that will be affected by the change. Pay attention to those who seem hesitant and take their concerns seriously.

Change management is "people management" because you have to deal with people at each stage of the process. How you handle people will determine their level of commitment to the change process. You have to come up with effective strategies on how to deal with the inevitable resistance. Those who are being forced to adapt to the change are the ones who are most likely to resist it. A resistance management plan helps ensure that the change process is not delayed or sabotaged. The goal is to help others accept the transition and reduce the risk of resistance. Keep the communication channels open and work with them to develop practical solutions and strategies.

Step 2: Create a Plan

Once you've clearly articulated the need for change and the organization has embraced your vision, you need to create an action plan. The plan is based on the goals of the change initiative. It must be thorough enough to provide a detailed, step-by-step sequence of activities for executing change. It must also be realistic by outlining a workable timeline for the transition. This will ensure optimal use of available resources with minimal disruption and inefficiencies.

A change plan usually contains the following four elements:

Strategic Goals

Your plan must be clear on the goals that the change seeks to achieve for the organization. By setting strategic goals, you will influence how your team utilizes its energy and resources. You don't want your team to have mixed or misplaced priorities during the change process. That's like playing a chess game with no clear game plan. Imagine your pieces scattered all over the board with every piece going wherever it wants. You'll get destroyed by your opponent! Your project team should have concrete objectives to focus on and keep them motivated. Don't forget that strategic goals must include quantifiable or qualitative metrics to enable you to measure the results.

Key Performance Indicators (KPIs)

These are critical indicators used to measure the effectiveness of your team in achieving a goal. When setting up KPIs, first establish the baseline for the status quo. This will give you something to compare your results against. Then, you need to describe what a successful change will look like and how it should be measured. Finally, set targets for performance and then track your progress against the target.

Stakeholders and Team

You need to determine the specific roles and responsibilities of the people involved in implementing the change. For example, who will supervise the change process? What activity is each individual or team responsible for? Who has to sign off at each phase of the change? One of the biggest sources of change resistance is ambiguity, especially disorganization in the change project team. When people are not sure of their role, they end up stepping on each other's toes.

You need to minimize the ambiguity that often comes with change. One way to do this is through effective and timely communication. Everyone's roles should be assigned from the beginning to avoid confusion or conflict during the change process. At a minimum, your change management team should include a cross-section of people from across the organization. Select people who have the right skills and experience for the roles they're supposed to play. Team members must also have a clear picture of every stage of the process. They should be capable influencers who can lobby and negotiate on behalf of the project.

There should also be clear communication of progress, strategies, and outcomes with all relevant stakeholders. Ensure that relevant messages are communicated early to prevent the risk of rumors. If there is a failure during the project, be open about it. Your goal should be to provide people with information even when you don't have all the answers. Use a variety of available media channels and techniques to send out messages consistently. Transparency and exchange of feedback help build trust with stakeholders. It also encourages your team to feel invested in the change.

Scope

Scope covers the steps and actions that are part of the change process. Creating a well-defined scope is one way to ensure the success of your change initiative. Without a project scope, you will struggle to implement change no matter how efficient or effective your team is. The scope enables you to assign resources and create reasonable timelines for your project. It allows the project team to know the deliverables required, thus providing direction for employees. The scope also outlines the skills required by team members as well as potential constraints. It's also a good idea to highlight the areas that are not within the scope of the project to avoid wasting resources.

Sometimes, you may need to change certain aspects of the scope. However, avoid reworking the scope of the project as this will force you to invest more resources. If you have to adjust something, limit it, and make sure you consider the opinions of stakeholders and employees involved in the project. This will help you avoid disagreements later on.

Step 3: Implement the Changes

Once you have created the plan, the next step is to follow it and implement the change. This is where the real work of change management starts. You have to break down the plan into smaller tasks to make the individual targets more achievable and easier to manage. During the implementation phase, it's important to maintain communication with staff members. Encourage teams to collaborate and keep communication channels open. You don't want a situation where some employees are struggling with a task, yet the change managers are oblivious to it.

You should also consider whether to pilot the change before going full throttle. You can implement the change on a small scale for a fixed period and then review the results. This is usually a good way to show the benefits of the change to those who are still unconvinced. When people see the progress made on a small scale, they gain the motivation and momentum to fully embrace the change.

As implementation continues, change managers should focus on empowering employees to stay on track with set goals. The change management plan should be rigorously monitored, frequently updated, and communicated to assigned teams and individuals. There should be regular project meetings to discuss updates and action items in the plan. Sometimes, there will be changes to the original plan, for example, a reassignment of task owners or supervisors. This information should be added to the plan in the form of comments and shared with all relevant stakeholders.

There are always obstacles that threaten the change process, so make sure that these are prevented or mitigated the moment they are identified. If the change is related to the organization's systems, strategies, or processes, it may be necessary to implement training or upskilling of employees. This will prepare them to adapt to the new environment.

Step 4: Embed the Changes

It's one thing to implement a change in an organization. But ensuring that everyone embraces or adapts to it instead of reverting to the status quo is a different thing altogether. Embedding changes within the organization's culture is important, especially if they are related to workflows, strategies, and culture. In many cases, employees are tempted to backslide to their former way of doing things. This is a real threat in the transition period after a change has been implemented.

One of the things that contribute to this problem is the lack of a comprehensive plan to embed change. Some leaders do not take it as seriously as the design or implementation plan. It is easy to fall into the trap of

CHANGE WIZARD | 125

believing that once the change is well-executed, things will be bright and rosy. Leaders often see a vanilla future and quickly move on to the next shiny goal.

To effectively embed changes in an organization's culture, you must establish control mechanisms. You need to continually evaluate what's working and what's not during the transition period. Monitor and record the results of the change as well as the behavior of employees. If there is an area that isn't working well, improvements should be made. You should also consider reward systems to entice employees to stick to the change. But ultimately, the best way to embed change is through employee empowerment. When employees buy into and become emotionally connected to the change, they will see it as part of their self-expression at work. Help your employees take owner-ship of the change, and it will effectively be embedded into the organization.

Step 5: Review Progress and Results

A change initiative cannot be deemed successful just because the project is complete. You can only deter-mine whether it was a success or not after undertaking a thorough review and analysis. But wholesale success or failure are not the only outcomes you may contend with. A review can also help you determine whether the outcome is a mixed result, i.e., you succeeded in some areas but failed in others. The information provides valuable lessons and insights that can be used to improve change projects in the future. This shows you just how important it is to conduct a thorough post-implementation review. It can make the difference between executing change the right way and repeating the mistakes of the past.

The post-implementation review should be conducted during the closing stages of the change initiative. It should involve the analysis of project performance against the original goals of the change initiative. The review also ensures that there is a constant improvement of deliverables from the change management team. With every successful review conducted, change team members become the go-to experts within the organization.

Your post-implementation review should include:

- Review of the project goals
- Evaluation of whether timelines were kept
- Identification of challenges that impacted the outcome and how to address them in the future
- Lessons learned, for example, unforeseen risks and costs
- Any feedback from the change management team

The effort you put into your review will depend on several factors. If you were running a pilot project, you need to expend a lot more effort on the review process because the information is going to be applied to the much larger change project. The same also applies if the project is a new initiative for your organization. Spend more resources to ensure your review is as detailed as possible so that you learn the right lessons.

Managing change effectively involves following a well-designed process and understanding every step along the way. Make sure that there is effective communication with everyone on the team and that regular evaluations are made during the process. As the change leader, you are accountable for the adoption and use of the implemented changes. Therefore, make sure that you design and begin with a proper plan and effective metrics.

KEY TAKEAWAYS

Here are five key action steps to take when designing the change process:

1. *Create specific goals.* Start by clearly defining your objectives. Ask yourself the five W's (who, why, what, which, and where). Who are the key players in the change process? Why is change

important? What tools will be needed to implement change? Which resources do you need? Where will the change project take place?

2. *Make your goals measurable.* Establish a baseline for the status quo to give you something to compare your results against. Clearly describe what a successful change will look like and the metrics to be used to measure progress. Don't forget to set project milestones and track your progress.

3. *Ensure that your goals are relevant to the organization.* Confirm whether the change aligns with organizational goals and strategy. Ask yourself these questions: "Is the change worthwhile?", "Does it match the needs of the organization?", "Are you the right person to lead this change?", and "Is it aligned with prevailing economic trends?".

4. *A change initiative must have a deadline and your goals must be time-related.* When should the change be complete? Be specific when providing a timeframe as time constraints help keep you on track.

5. *For your change plan to be complete, it must include a post-implementation review.* This will help you know whether project performance matches the original goals of the change initiative. How

will you collect feedback from stakeholders after the project? How do you intend to record the challenges and lessons learned? Clearly outline the methods you'll use to conduct this review.

It is important to design a comprehensive change process. This is not an easy thing to do, especially if you don't fully understand the principles that guide effective change management. In the next chapter, you will learn these principles in detail.

THE 10 PRINCIPLES OF CHANGE MANAGEMENT

M ost leaders prefer having a stable environment to work in. They prioritize stability in their organization so that staff members can focus on their work and stay productive. A stable organization is also good for investors and shareholders who want to earn predictable yet growing returns. Customers want to buy from companies that have stable and trustworthy leadership. These are the kinds of companies that provide innovative and high-quality products and services to customers.

Customers respond well to companies that offer them goods and services that solve their problems. They vote with their wallets and the constant flow of revenue ensures that the company stays profitable. Investors reap good returns, employees earn good salaries, and senior executives earn their bonuses. All this is a result of having stability in an organization.

As you can see, having a stable working environment in an organization is beneficial for all stakeholders concerned. This kind of business environment was easy to deliver decades ago. If any changes were made within an organization, they were modest and infrequent. Those were the good ol' days when people stayed in one job for life and product prices were stable.

But those days are gone, and it's highly unlikely that they'll ever be back. We now live in a world where labor mobility, wild price swings, increased global competition, and market disruptions have become the norm. Almost every industry has been affected, and no organization can sit comfortably any longer. Leaders of companies are now forced to contend with one thing they would rather avoid — change. They have to keep adapting and evolving just to keep up with the competition.

Most business leaders face a challenge when dealing with how to adopt change. When undertaking major transformations, they tend to focus primarily on creating strategic plans. They forget that a great plan is nothing without people. A good plan still needs the collective, persistent actions of employees who are expected to execute and adapt to the change. If you want to succeed in implementing change, you must understand the "people" aspect of change management. Change can only be embedded if it is embraced at the level of the individual employee.

This is something that worries many leaders who are involved in organizational transformation. They worry about how their workforce will respond and whether employees can work together to adopt the change. There is also the fear of losing the organization's unique culture and identity. As a leader, you need to plan for the human aspect of change management. To do this, you must understand the principles that guide effective change management. Here are 10 principles that can help you manage and engage your workforce in the change process:

1. Address the Human Element Thoroughly

There is no way that you can introduce change to an organization without encountering "people" issues. For example, individuals who may have been in the periphery may be asked to step into the limelight. Roles and responsibilities may be transferred. Employees may be asked to learn new skills. Some staff members may be uncomfortable with the changes that are happening. You cannot afford to be reactive to these issues as they may jeopardize the implementation of change.

Employee morale and the pace of adoption will be at risk.

This is why you need to develop a comprehensive plan early on. Your change management plan should involve the leadership team, change champions, and key stakeholders. It should be a flexible plan that adapts to any issues that arise during the implementation phase. Collect and analyze data that reflects the current state of the culture, attitudes, and behavior of the workforce. This information will guide you on how to settle any issues that may threaten the change process.

There must be a high level of discipline when it comes to developing and implementing the change management plan. It must be integrated into the project design and used when determining change strategies. It should also be an accurate assessment of the history, capacity, and preparedness of your organization.

2. Lead from the Front

When things become confusing and anxiety runs high, people always look to their leader for support, strength, and direction. This is evident during times of transition because change has a way of upsetting people. As a leader, you are expected to be one of the first people to embrace the change. Doing so challenges and motivates your workforce to at least contemplate the change and its intended benefits.

The leadership team must also display a unity of purpose and speak with one voice. They must model the changes they want the rest of the organization to adopt. Some within the leadership team may have reservations about the change. They may be just as stressed and unsettled as other employees. If this happens, offer them the support they need to embrace the change.

Success can only be achieved if the leadership team works together and is fully committed to steering the change in the right direction. Failure to do so paints a negative and confusing picture to employees, and they may resist the change. Don't assume that you can start the initiative with gusto and then your employees will keep the ball rolling as you focus on other things. The moment your workforce begins to question your commitment, they will lose interest and fail to deliver results. A leader's vision and commitment to the change initiative should be consistent from start to finish.

3. Involve Every Level of the Organization

A change initiative is going to affect different levels of the organization. Knowing this, you must identify and involve individuals at every level from the moment you begin designing the change plan. Find change leaders at every layer of the organization and give them the responsibility to design and implement change downward. This can effectively ensure that change flows throughout the organization. These change leaders must be trained and aligned to the organization's vision. They should also be empowered and motivated with the tools they need to execute their specific mandate.

By following a cascading leadership approach, teams at all levels and layers of the organization can take ownership of the change initiative. For example, executives and managers can design the fundamentals of the change initiative. Mid-level officers can then establish the vision, strategies, and targets. Front-line leaders can drive the implementation process. This is an effective way to identify future leaders within the organization. This methodology is also more likely to generate success than if senior management designed everything and then left the implementation work to their subordinates.

4. Articulate a Formal Case for Change

Trying to introduce change in an organization is going to lead to questions. People will want to know the scope and scale of the changes, whether they are necessary and if they are good for everyone in the company. How you make your argument for change will determine whether people support and commit to the change initiative. Instead of perceiving this as a nuisance, see it as an invaluable opportunity to align your vision with that of your team.

There are three steps you should take when making a case for change. First, confront reality and convince people of the necessity for change. Secondly, express confidence that the organization is on the right path and has capable leadership at the helm. Finally, you need to show that you have a clear plan to guide behavior, performance, and decision-making. Once you have successfully completed these steps, you can move on to selling the change to the individual departments within the organization.

Each of the above steps is important in its own way and serves a unique purpose. For example, some departments in the organization will need more convincing because the change may disrupt their operations more than others. You need to project enough confidence to show them that there is a clear plan in place and senior leadership is on top of everything. To achieve this, you may need to tackle each relevant department as an individual layer.

Think of each department as a layer of the organization. Each has its internal audience. For example, the way you make your case to the marketing team is not the way you articulate your message to the human resources department. Customize your argument for each of them so that you can describe the change in a way that's relevant to every group.

5. Create Ownership

For a change program to be successful, it must have a critical mass of people who support the transformation. It's not enough to have a passive buy-in from the workforce. There has to be active and zealous support throughout the organization. At every level of the organization, you must have leaders who can accept responsibility for implementing the change in their area of influence. This is referred to as *creating ownership*. You create ownership for change by involving people from the beginning of the process. When key stakeholders feel included, it can create a kind of unity that may not have existed before in the organization.

You should allow departmental leaders to identify problems that they see and their relevant solutions. You can also use rewards and incentives to reinforce a sense of ownership. The incentives need not be financial. Psychological incentives, such as a sense of shared purpose or comradeship, can also work.

6. Communicate the Message of Change

One of the errors that leaders often make when undertaking a change initiative is assuming that everyone will understand its need. They mistakenly believe that others will see issues as they do and embrace the new direction. This rarely happens.

What defines a good change initiative is the way the message is communicated by the change leader. The best approach is to communicate the core message regularly and promptly. Reinforce the change message in a way that is inspirational and practical. Employees should be provided with the right information when they need it, and their feedback must be solicited and considered. This may often require that you broadcast the message using multiple channels of communication.

Let's say you want to change the culture of your organization and transform the attitude of your employees. A system or process redesign is not going to be enough to get hundreds, maybe thousands, of people to change the way they think and act. This is a mindset change, and you have to engage with people at the individual level to successfully embed this kind of shift. Change leaders must communicate continually with the workforce and encourage them to embrace the transformation. You can do this through group chats, daily emails, newsletters, training sessions, and meetings. Keep reinforcing the message until the transformation happens.

7. Consider the Organizational Culture

For a successful change initiative, there needs to be an increase in the speed and intensity of adoption as it makes its way down the organization. But this can only happen if the culture and behavior of the employees are aligned with the change. This is why leaders must always assess and understand the existing culture within the organization before adopting a change program.

Most companies realize the importance of a cultural assessment only when it's too late. Some never realize it at all. But a systematic cultural assessment is beneficial because it shows you whether the organization is ready for change. It also highlights any unseen issues that may hinder the change process, such as potential conflicts and sources of resistance. On the flip side, a cultural assessment also reveals individuals that can be relied on as change leaders. A cultural analysis shows you what the core values and beliefs are, and the perceptions people have. This information is crucial for designing the various elements of change.

8. Address Cultural Issues Directly

After identifying and assessing the existing culture, you should address it openly and thoroughly. You should communicate how the present culture is ineffective in achieving the goals of the organization. Once you do this, create a baseline, and explicitly define what the desired culture should look like. Then design a detailed plan of how the organization is going to make that transition. As a leader, make it clear that there must be a new culture that supports the new way of doing things. You also need to find ways of modeling the cultural change you want to see and rewarding those who comply.

Every organization has its unique cultural center which often defines the thoughts, actions, and identities of employees. This culture is formed through a combination of explicit values, common behaviors, and a shared history. However, once you understand the culture, you can transform it in several ways. You can create a new one, for example, when starting a new company. You can also combine cultures such as during mergers and acquisitions.

9. Expect the Unexpected

Murphy's Law says that if there is a chance that something will go wrong, it will. This law applies to change management too. A change initiative can go completely off-script. Employees may react unexpectedly. Those who resist may decide to support change while some who supported it may turn against it. The business environment may also shift unexpectedly, yet your plan relies on market factors staying the same.

To effectively manage change, you must be prepared to continually re-evaluate your plan. You must keep an eye out for the next wave that may influence your plan and assess whether the organization can adapt. The good news is that you are not working blind. Use the data coming from the front lines and combine it with sound decision-making processes. This will help you make the right adjustments to keep the change process on track.

10. Connect to the Individual

Change happens at the organizational as well as the individual level. Some people regard their workmates as a second family, and any change at work raises tension and questions. They want to know how the change will affect their work and what the new expectations are. They want to know the consequences of success or failure both for them and their colleagues. Therefore, change leaders should speak explicitly to the person's concerns.

People will wait to see how the change process affects them on an individual level. For example, what happens to those who embrace change quickly? You can offer them rewards, such as bonuses or promotions, as a way to encourage others. Alternatively, you can penalize or remove individuals who are obstacles to change. Make sure that these actions are done openly to show the organization's commitment to change.

KEY TAKEAWAYS:

Here are five steps to take to implement the principles of change management:

1. *Change is driven by people.* Therefore, you must be prepared to deal with the myriad issues that people have, especially during a transition. Take the time to talk to people at all levels of the organization and pay attention to their concerns. Adopt a coaching leadership style by having personal meetings with stakeholders. Balance your praise and criticism when speaking to employees. Respect them, and they will trust in your leadership.

2. *Your organization's culture will show you how people will respond to change.* Therefore, you must explore key attributes of the organization such as leadership involvement, decision-making processes, and communication channels. How

do leaders relate to their subordinates? Do leaders say one thing and do the opposite? Do all stakeholders have a say or do the executives make flat decisions? What means of communication are used, and how open are the communication channels?

3. *Your front-line workers must feel that they own the change process.* After all, they bear the greatest burden of implementing the change initiative. Make sure you collect their input and incorporate it into the change plan. Use financial rewards or publicly appreciate employees who are performing well in the change initiative.

4. *Involve individuals at every level of the organization when designing the change plan.* First, identify change champions and give them the responsibility to design and implement change downward. Senior managers can design the fundamentals of the change initiative. Mid-level officers should establish the strategies and targets, and front-line leaders can drive the implementation process. Offer them the necessary training and tools to execute their mandate. Ensure prompt and effective communication via group chats, daily emails, and newsletters to spread the message of

change. Hold training sessions and meetings where you can boldly articulate the case for change. Also, encourage employees to provide feedback using available communication channels.

5. *Always have a backup plan or at least be flexible enough to adjust the original plan.* Environments change, and so do people. Sit down with various stakeholders and brainstorm on any potential setbacks you may experience. Then, pencil in solutions to probable challenges into your plan. This way, you aren't caught totally off guard when the unexpected happens.

You will encounter some obstacles when implementing change. Sometimes, you will be forced to use the stick rather than the carrot. In the next chapter, you will learn how to be decisive and tough-minded when executing change.

HOW TO BE DECISIVE AND TOUGH-MINDED

A change process is designed to replace or adjust an existing system. Since people tend to get comfortable with what they already have, trying to change things can make you quite unpopular. But as a leader, you have to be ready and willing to go against the grain when making decisions.

Let's take the example of Jeff Bezos. He launched Amazon.com in 1995 as an online bookstore at a time when people were still buying books from physical stores. This was a bold move to make, and initially, Amazon struggled to make profits. Yet Bezos took this decisive step and stuck to his guns. Within two years, Amazon had diversified and was selling a range of products. Today, it is the largest online retailer and one of the most valuable companies in the world.

According to Bezos, a leader must be stubborn in their vision but flexible with the details. Being stubborn helps you stay persistent during challenges while being flexible helps you find new solutions to existing problems. In this chapter, you will learn some of the qualities that define a decisive and tough-minded leader. You will also learn some key strategies on how to develop these traits.

WHY YOU NEED TO BE DECISIVE AND TOUGH-MINDED

To execute change in an organization, you must be willing to take bold and calculated risks. You must also have the capacity to withstand resistance without buckling under pressure. Being decisive and tough-minded are important qualities that every leader must develop.

But what does it mean to be decisive and tough-minded?

To be decisive means to be firm, resolute, and determined. A decisive person displays little to no hesitation when making a decision. They make their decision quickly and take immediate action. This is an important quality of effective leadership, especially during times of great uncertainty and volatility. This does not mean that a decisive leader makes rash and unsubstantiated decisions. A good leader will always consult others and take the time to gather as much relevant information as possible. However, a decisive leader does not wait around to have all the available information. They make the best decision based on what they know.

A tough-minded individual has a strong will and doesn't change their mind easily once it's made up. They are practical and avoid sentimentality when making decisions. They dare to initiate tough conversations to find the right solutions. When it's time to put an end to a debate, they do so quickly and directly to move their team forward. Tough-minded leaders are viewed as reliable and strong by their colleagues.

A leader needs to embrace both qualities because having one without the other can lead to problems in the organization. Take the example of a CEO who is decisive but not tough-minded. The organization is facing an urgent financial crisis and after evaluating several solutions, they quickly select the best one. However, some managers complain about the decision. The CEO backs down and makes an alternative decision. Then, another group of managers complains about the second decision and the CEO goes back to the initial decision. This symbolizes a leader who is decisive but lacks tough-mindedness. They are constantly flip-flopping from one position to the next — being pushed around too easily. This creates chaos and confusion in the organization.

On the other hand, a leader may be tough-minded but indecisive. When an urgent financial crisis hits the organization, they avoid making a quick decision. They stubbornly say that they need to have all the information before taking any action. As they do this, the company reels under financial pressure, and employees begin to lose faith in their leadership. When the CEO finally does something, it turns out to be the same old decision made during previous financial challenges. After all the waiting and consulting, the CEO stubbornly refuses to make a new decision and opts for old solutions. Employees are left frustrated because they were expecting a dynamic or innovative solution that would fix the problem long term. Unfortunately, the company ends up doing the same things over and over, and each bad decision precipitates the next crisis.

When you learn how to be decisive and tough-minded, you reap the benefits of both. Being decisive enables you to make quick and timely decisions when necessary. This is very important at a time when the business landscape is shifting rapidly with organizations struggling to keep up. There are times when you don't have all the information you need. You may also not have full consensus from your team. But you must be prepared to make a quick decision regardless of the situation.

At the same time, being tough-minded helps you stick to your decision in the face of resistance. Those who are not happy with your decision may try to sway you to change your mind. Some people may resort to emotive arguments that have no substance. But a tough-minded leader understands the need for practicality and rigorous thinking to confront such flawed arguments.

Developing these traits earns you the respect of your team. You are viewed as a leader who quickly marshals the troops to come up with ideas, chooses the best one, and then follows through on it. Being decisive and tough-minded also enhances transparency and clarity. When you stand by a decision, you also have to explain to your team why you're doing so and what your intentions are. You can offer clear instructions without your employees worrying whether you're going to change your mind. A decisive and tough-minded leader makes their team feel part of the decision-making process. This enhances cohesion and unity of purpose.

It's important to note that there's a thin line between being tough-minded and being stubborn. Though you don't want to be swayed by sentimental or impractical ideas, you should always consider what others have to say. A stubborn person usually rejects all advice and does whatever they want to protect their fragile ego. This does not reflect good leadership.

DECISIVENESS IS A PROCESS

Business is now being conducted at a faster pace than ever before. Coupled with increasing time pressures, it's becoming more of a challenge to deal with the complexity and speed of change. In such an environment, leaders are required to make the best decisions possible within a short period. They are judged by whether those choices help or hurt their organization.

During times of uncertainty, the best leaders are those who make strong and defensible decisions timely. At every level of an organization, managers are constantly making decisions that determine the fate of the organization. Any leader who is seen as indecisive quickly loses their team's confidence and commitment. Any leader who makes quick, yet unsound decisions is judged to be a failure.

But how do you ensure that you have a higher percentage of good decisions than bad ones?

It's all about perspective. Good leaders perceive decision-making as a process rather than an event. Following this process enables you to avoid the pitfalls of taking too long and the dangers of deciding too quickly.

This process has the following seven steps:

Step 1: Gather Information

The first thing to do is collect information from a wide range of sources. Studies show that an average leader who has access to diverse opinions will consistently make better decisions than the smartest CEO. Decisive leaders don't cocoon themselves in an echo chamber. They listen to as many diverse thoughts as possible, even if they differ from their own.

Step 2: Encourage Constructive Conflict

Conflict in an organization can be a positive thing as long as it occurs for the sake of collaboration and problem-solving. A leader should allow team members to share information widely and encourage diversity of opinion. There should be no selective cherry-picking of information to advance a particular position. Everyone must be allowed to evaluate all the information and draw conclusions. There should be no lobbying for entrenched positions as this may quickly lead to a contest where the dominant view wins. You don't want a situation where people go along with an idea just to avoid further conflict.

Step 3: Genuinely Consider the Alternatives

It's not enough for team members to give their thoughts and views. As a leader, you must honestly take into consideration the alternative views that they may offer. If your team feels that you never genuinely considered or heard their voices, they may rebel against the change process. It's also true that considering multiple alternatives fosters a more thoughtful assessment. It prevents you from settling on the obvious solution too early. Therefore, a leader must show openness through active listening and seriously evaluating the alternative solutions provided.

Step 4: Avoid Dominating the Process

Leaders tend to have a lot of influence over their followers. They always speak first and the most, regardless of the group they are in. A leader can easily shape the collective opinion of a group even if their message makes little to no sense. The likelihood of this happening increases if the leader has a charismatic personality. When leading a decision-making process, avoid slanting the debate in your favor. Don't inform the team about your personal preferences early in the process. If you do, the team may simply rubber-stamp your ideas instead of engaging in a constructive debate.

Step 5: Test Your Assumptions

There is a difference between ideas that have been carefully tested and those that are mere assumptions. Test your assumptions by seeking out people who have a contrary opinion. They may ask hard questions that reveal flaws in your plan.

Step 6: Thoroughly Explain Your Decision

Once you've settled on a clear decision, mobilize resources, and take action. This will help give credibility to your decision. However, it's also a good idea to explain to your team the thought process that led to your final decision. Let them know how their input influenced the decision. Keep in mind that people process information differently, so communicate clearly and concisely to avoid any ambiguity.

Step 7: Stay Engaged During Implementation

A good decision is worth nothing if it's poorly executed. It won't even matter how much effort went into the decision-making process — it will still be a poor decision. A decisive leader continues to engage with the change process by asking for regular feedback and providing active support. You should also be prepared to make adjustments to your initial plan.

HOW TO MAKE DECISIONS FASTER

As much as we may place focus on following a decision-making process, we must acknowledge the reality on the ground. In the real world, you may not have the luxury of evaluating every possible alternative. You may not have enough time to get the opinions of every stakeholder. To be an effective leader, sometimes you have to make some tough calls on your own.

However, there are strategies that you can use to help you become more confident when making decisions quickly. Here are five steps you can take to make the best decision as fast as possible.

Step 1: Trust Your Gut

When trying to make a decision, we often rely on what we know or see. We lean toward logic and rational analysis because we live in a data-driven world. Everywhere you look, you are inundated with number-crunching algorithms that help you make decisions. Whether it's who to hire, who to date, or what to invest in, we are increasingly becoming slaves to quantifiable data.

But your body also has internal algorithms for processing data and interpreting information. This is your gut instinct. With studies now showing that your gut is like a second brain, it makes sense why many successful leaders say that they rely on their intuition for decision-making. Despite having access to lots of empirical data, over 40% of CEOs claim that they still rely on their gut to make decisions.

This doesn't mean you should discard empirical information. It's all about learning how to balance between your gut feeling and analytical data. When you have to make a quick decision, you may not have time to go through all the charts and reports placed in front of you. A good old-fashioned gut check can help you know what to do or not do when facing a dicey situation.

Your gut instinct has evolved over millions of years as a way of sending signals even before the rational mind knows what's happening. But trusting your instincts can be difficult in a culture where rationality seems to be the highest ideal. Business leaders often prioritize quantifiable metrics instead of trying to understand their customers' subconscious motives.

So, how do you learn how to trust your instincts?

The first thing to realize is that your gut instinct is highly individual. A person may get a knot in their stomach. Another may feel a headache or have tense shoulders. You need to be self-aware to know how your body speaks to you. The good news is that the more situations you face over time, the more you learn how your instincts work. With every experience you face, whether negative or positive, you will gradually learn to listen and trust your instincts.

Trusting your instincts means paying attention to yourself. All you have to do is pay attention to the signals your body is sending you in various situations. By reflecting on an outcome, you can discern the underlying thoughts and emotions that you felt at the time. Self-reflection is very important during this process. It requires you to be still and review the decisions you've made during your day. You must do this with both good and bad decisions.

For example, when a decision turns out to be a good one, reflect on how you felt before you made that call. If a decision turns out negatively, try to remember any warning sensations you felt. Over time, you'll start recognizing patterns in how your gut communicates to you. You can learn to trust your instinct through mindfulness techniques, meditation, and even yoga. These techniques teach you to slow down and truly listen to your body.

Another way to trust your instincts is to back it up with research. Instead of trying to convince board members about how your gut has been right in the past, walk into the meeting armed with hard numbers and analysis. Use reports and analytics to support your assertions. A panel of advisors can also be useful when you need people to listen to your instinctual ideas. They may pinpoint a flaw or support your idea as a good solution.

Step 2: Think About the Big Picture

To make a quick decision with confidence, you need to consider its long-term impact. In most cases, we tend to make decisions by focusing only on the short-term outcome. We get so embroiled in the daily grind of work that we forget about the long-term objective. Therefore, a decision that appears to be a good one today may turn out to be a bad one later on.

Studies show that you make the most efficient decisions when you look at the bigger picture. As a leader, you must ensure that your decisions create the greatest value for your organization. This means taking a step back and assessing how that decision will impact the organization in the future. For example, how will the change you're making affect the business a year from now? How will it affect the long-term operations of your team?

By consistently thinking about the big picture, you gradually learn how to make the best decisions possible. Every decision you make is then aligned with the long-term objectives of the organization. When you have to make a quick decision, you'll automatically know which ideas to consider and the ones to discard.

Step 3: Act as if You Are Advising a Friend

As a leader, you spend a lot of time advising others and telling them what to do. However, you need to learn to do the opposite whenever you're faced with a tough decision. If you have to make a quick decision, assume it's a friend who's asking for your insight. What kind of advice would you give them? What compelling reasons would you give to support their idea? How would you dissuade them from moving forward with the idea?

By pretending to be advising someone else, you're avoiding any emotions that may be attached to the decision. Emotions can cloud your judgment and make it much harder to make a good decision quickly. Alternatively, you can seek out a trusted colleague or mentor and ask them for their opinion. Sometimes, an external party may provide fresh insight that helps you see things you never considered before.

Step 4: Restrict Your Information

To most people, a decision is best made when you have as much information as possible. However, sometimes limiting the information you have to study can be the best option. This is especially true when you have to make a quick decision.

"Paralysis analysis" is one of the things that hinder quick and effective decision-making. When you have too much data and details to read through, your brain simply becomes overwhelmed by an information over-load. Unable to think properly, you freeze in your tracks. You may end up sifting through tons of infor-mation that have nothing to do with the decision you need to make. You may also miss some crucial data because there was too much information to go through within a short period.

You have to find a balance that works. One way to do this is to limit the amount of information you need. As long as the information is relevant to your decision, it will help you come to a timely resolution. For example, you can choose three of the most recent market research reports instead of trying to read through every available one.

Step 5: Use a Visual Approach

Some people are more visual in the way they process information. They prefer to use graphs, charts, and pictures when evaluating ideas. Instead of reading through tons of literature and writing down your ideas, draw them. Use diagrams and tables to describe the different factors that are influencing your decisions. You can also perform a SWOT (strengths, weaknesses, opportunities, and threats) analysis to determine how effective your idea will be in achieving the goal. You may also discover that visual aids are more effective at helping you see the bigger picture.

QUALITIES OF A DECISIVE LEADER

Having a decisive personality affects your life both within and outside the workplace. In any situation, your ability to decide is critical. Whether you're deciding who to hire, what to have for dinner, or how to handle your teenager, there can be no action without clear decisions. If you cannot make decisions with speed and clarity, your life is likely to stagnate, and you won't achieve your potential.

But why do some individuals choose to be indecisive?

Unfortunately, some people consider being indecisive as an effective strategy for solving their problems. For example, a leader may behave indecisively because they don't want to shoulder the burden of making a tough decision. They assume that if they procrastinate, something or someone else will decide for them. This may seem like the easy way out of a problem, but it makes you appear weak to others.

Being a decisive leader doesn't mean you have to come up with a solution immediately. It can be as simple as deciding to do more research or consult your advisors. Leadership is defined by your ability to make important decisions and then act on them. Therefore, a decisive leader has specific qualities that separate them from an indecisive one. Here are four traits of a decisive leader:

Confidence

A decisive leader is bold and courageous in their decisions and actions. Even when they have little information available, they take a course of action to move the organization forward. They do not fear uncertainty or risks because they know that very few decisions are ever made based on complete information. In a world full of uncertainty, confidence in decision-making makes a big difference.

Confidence is also necessary when making a decision that is unpopular with sections of the workforce. You either stick to your guns or be swayed by the people around you. You shouldn't be meek or blasé about things. This doesn't mean you should bulldoze others and ignore their input. However, you must project confidence to your team to dispel any notion that you're simply dabbling.

Resilience

Once they've made up their mind, a decisive leader does not rush to change it. They know that the decision was based on information they had available at the time. It's also likely that they consulted others before deciding on a course of action. Unless there's a major unforeseen problem, a decisive leader sticks to their decision. By resisting the pressure to change their decision unnecessarily, a leader stamps their authority and lets doubters know that they are fully in charge.

Accountability

A decisive leader makes decisions quickly and holds themselves and their team accountable for the outcome. Since the spring of 2020, we have seen how various world leaders have handled the COVID-19 pandemic and the economic decline of their nations. Whereas some were quick to act, others adopted a wait-and-see approach and paid the price for it. As always, indecisive leaders refuse to accept responsibility or admit their mistakes.

Taking ownership is a critical aspect of leadership. If you are leading an organization, you must be ready to be held responsible for the choices you make. A decisive leader understands this and isn't afraid of facing such commitments. They are comfortable with the risk that comes with decisiveness, especially if it's an informed risk.

Sense of Urgency

Research shows that organizations are struggling to keep pace with changes occurring around the world. This rapid rate of change will only increase over time. Therefore, leaders must create a sense of urgency to avoid being left behind. A decisive leader takes steps to get the attention of major stakeholders in the organization. They don't waste time communicating the need for rapid changes to the status quo.

Creating a sense of urgency is important because you need the cooperation of all relevant stakeholders. You must convince them that the status quo is dangerous and there's greater value in transforming the organization. Have an honest conversation with them about the current market, available opportunities, potential crises, and competitive realities.

Make sure that the leadership shows serious commitment to change by first stopping the waste of resources. Openly share any data that supports the need for change, even if it's bad news about the organization. Encourage managers and supervisors to talk to other employees, suppliers, and clients about any concerns they may have about the business. Finally, ensure that decisions made and actions taken by the leadership align with the change being communicated.

PITFALLS TO WATCH OUT FOR

As a leader, being decisive boosts the confidence and efficiency of your team. However, there are also some pitfalls of a decisive personality trait. This is why you need to have a high sense of self-awareness. You need to understand your personality and how it affects those around you. You should also learn to identify a decisive personality among your team members as this can affect relationships within your team.

One of the qualities you should watch out for is impatience. Decisive people tend to get impatient when they are faced with delays or inefficiencies. They don't understand why things aren't moving at their pace. Since their minds work faster than other people, they expect everyone around them to keep up. If you're a decisive leader, you have to know when to slow down and loop in the rest of the team.

Decisive people should be attentive to how they communicate with peers who are less decisive. Don't forget that implementing change in an organization is a team effort. People have different communication styles, and you must learn how to relate to everyone at their level. You don't want to come across as being someone who steamrolls others and denies them the chance to contribute their ideas. Sometimes, you have to slow down and explain things so that others can catch up.

Decisive leaders also get frustrated easily when they feel the decision-making process is taking too long. Let's say you want to implement changes but the final decision rests with senior executives. Due to their busy schedules, they may take their time to approve the changes. In the meantime, you're pulling out your hair waiting for them to get back to you. If the process is taking too long, ask to be kept in the loop as you wait.

You also need to know how to handle employees who have decisive personalities. Apart from providing them with regular feedback during delays, consider recruiting them for roles that require independent decision-making. This will help the team maximize their decisive nature. You may also need to remind them of times in the past when they benefited from making decisions more slowly.

HOW TO BE A COLLABORATIVE DECISION-MAKER

There is an African proverb that says, "If you want to go fast, go alone. If you want to go far, go together." It implies that anyone who wants to achieve a goal quickly should do it alone. However, working by yourself can leave you weary and worn. At the same time, you're more likely to accomplish greater things if you have people around you who support your mission. The reality is that you don't have to choose one over the other. Both approaches have their benefits. However, leading an organization is a big responsibility with a lot of pressure. You must collaborate with others to carry out the myriad tasks that keep an organization moving forward.

Leaders who have adopted a collaborative approach to decision-making understand the importance of valuing, respecting, and listening to people. When employees feel involved in the decision-making process, they buy into the organization's goals and take ownership of delivering results. Collaborative decision-making makes it easier to streamline systems and processes in a company, improving long-term profitability and performance.

Since leadership is about people management, it's important to understand how people make decisions. There are three ways in which an individual makes a decision:

1. **Personal interest reasoning:** This is where an individual makes decisions based on ego, self-interest, or risk-avoidance. A person is

primarily motivated to seek pleasure and avoid pain.

2. **Normative reasoning:** The individual doesn't want to challenge the status quo. They make decisions that follow the existing rules and norms.

3. **Complex moral reasoning:** The individual is motivated to make decisions by using a collaborative and social cooperation approach. They recognize and consider other people's rights and want to ensure that every decision is fair.

This book is about learning how to embrace change. You cannot do this effectively if you are selfish, risk-averse, or afraid of challenging the status quo. You need to avoid personal interest and normative reasoning when making decisions. Therefore, complex moral reasoning is the way to go.

In society, it's a well-known fact that women tend to be more collaborative than men when making decisions. Coincidentally, research shows that women make better decisions for their companies, especially when there are competing interests involved. In a survey of more than 600 board members, it was revealed that women tend to consider the rights of others and adopt a collaborative approach when making decisions.

168 | MARLENE GONZALEZ

Female leaders tend to be more considerate of multiple stakeholders' interests and are more inclined to make moral and fair decisions. They prefer to build consensus rather than act as lone rangers. Whereas the male directors in the survey preferred to make decisions based on traditional rules, their female counterparts were more willing to question the status quo (*Bart & McQueen, 2013*).

In a world where the business environment is changing faster than ever before, it may be more profitable to have more collaborative leaders. A study showed that companies that have more women on their boards had a 42% greater return on sales, a 66% higher return on capital, and a 53% higher return on equity (*Joy et al., 2007*). Working well with others when making decisions, especially at the top level, can lead to incredible gains for an organization. But being a collaborative decision-maker is a skill that anyone can learn regardless of gender. Here are four steps you can take to improve your collaborative decision-making:

Step 1: Take Your Time

When you're faced with a decision, allow yourself enough time to assess the situation. Assign a specific period for proper analysis and set a deadline for the decision to be made. Let your team and a trusted mentor know the timeframe so that they can hold you accountable to the deadline. If you're the type of person who avoids risk, ask your mentor to challenge you on it whenever you are procrastinating. Since they know you well, they can point out the reasons why you are delaying making a decision.

Step 2: Encourage Feedback

Ask your team to give you feedback whenever possible about the decisions you're making. This may not be easy at first because employees often shy away from speaking about the decisions a leader makes. This is especially true if the feedback is negative. Most employees will not willingly put their jobs on the line just to give their leader honest feedback.

If you want honest feedback from your employees, you must create an environment that is fair and transparent. There can be no fear of future retribution. Your employees must feel comfortable telling you the truth and pointing out some of the problems they see in the organization. But this kind of environment is only possible where there is openness, trust, and cooperation.

That's why part of your job as a leader is to create an environment of transparency and cooperation. You need to encourage various stakeholders to share their perspectives so that you have a broader perspective of things. Consult with the different departments in the organization. Marketing may have a different perspective than Human Resources. Research and Development may see things differently from Sales. By listening to as many distinct groups as possible, you can make a decision that is in everyone's best interests.

Step 3: Find Someone to Play the Devil's Advocate

A devil's advocate is someone who always offers a counter-narrative to the prevailing way of doing things. They argue against a position or decision to help determine its validity. You need a devil's advocate to challenge all the major decisions made in the organization. This can be one person or a team that examines a decision and tries to poke holes in it. Incorporate this into your monthly meetings to ensure that the decision-making process is as comprehensive and inclusive as possible.

Step 4: Understand Your Impact as a Decision-maker

A leader is expected to say what they mean and mean what they say. You don't have room to be vague or wishy-washy. You cannot hide behind fancy corporate rhetoric to avoid engaging with people on a personal level. If you're making decisions that affect the organization, you must spend time getting in touch with other departments. Get out of your comfort zone and engage with different projects as much as you can. Get to know employees at every level and treat them with consideration and respect.

It is increasingly necessary to be a decisive and tough-minded leader. The world over, organizations are desperate for leadership that is quick to respond, yet collaborative. People want leaders who are firm but fair and resolute yet adaptable. If you don't develop such skills, you can't provide the sound guidance and timely decisions that the people around you need. Learning to be decisive and tough-minded benefits everyone in the organization and secures your position as a leader.

KEY TAKEAWAYS

Here are five things to do to become a faster and more collaborative decision-maker:

1. *Develop self-awareness.* Take some time at the end of the day to write down how your day went. Perform a feedback analysis of the good and bad outcomes. Be honest with your emotions about these events. If something went badly, ask yourself why. If you made a bad decision, try to remember how you felt as you were making that decision. Did your gut instinct warn you, yet you ignored the feeling? Do the same for the positive events. Over time, you'll start to learn the patterns of how your gut instinct works.

2. *Learn to reflect on the big picture.* Spend time regularly asking yourself hard questions about your organization. Think about the kind of legacy your organization wants to have. Ask yourself whether your decisions and actions are aligned with that legacy. What adjectives would your customers, employees, and other stakeholders use to describe the impact of the organization? What images come to mind when you think about its legacy? Use these words and images as guides when making daily decisions at work.

3. *Perform a SWOT analysis using visual aids.* Gather your team for a brainstorming session. Collectively identify the best ideas for solving

the problem. Define the strengths, weaknesses, opportunities, and threats of each idea. What organizational resources and strengths do we have available to support this idea? Is it knowledge, skills, capital? What factors hinder or weaken our organization from implementing this idea? What opportunities exist in the market that this idea helps us maximize on? Are there factors that threaten the success of this idea? Support your arguments with graphs, charts, photos, etc., to make the analysis easier. Then narrow down the list and agree on the top three ideas as a team. For each idea, further define the strengths, weaknesses, opportunities, and threats. Use the findings to make your decision.

4. *Encourage feedback from your team.* Spend time meeting staff members in informal settings, such as during lunch, and ask them insightful questions. Ask them what changes they would make if they were in authority. What do they enjoy the least about their job? To prove your openness, start by taking action on small suggestions that employees have. You can also appoint some employees as feedback coaches to receive any grievances that other staff members

may have. You can shortlist some candidates and let employees choose whom they want.

5. *Learn to work with others as much as possible.* Join or create a small Mastermind group and meet weekly to share ideas and solve problems. Identify friends who are natural encouragers and meet with them regularly to support each other's goals and dreams. Find advisors and mentors who can answer your questions and provide advice when you're feeling stressed and under pressure.

In the next chapter, you will learn how to be more resolute and tenacious when dealing with resistance to change.

MAINTAINING DRIVE AND PERSISTENCE

The genesis of all change and transformation is the mind. Once you're mentally convinced that change is the only way to go, making a forward leap becomes much easier. Unfortunately, getting to that mindset is easier said than done. The mind resists change, and people often quit on their journey of transformation because they couldn't adjust their mindset.

Of course, this becomes much more apparent when you're trying to implement change in an organization. Whereas personal change requires you to contend with your mind, organizational change involves dealing with resistance from multiple sources. You're forced to cope with the thoughts and feelings of everyone in the organization, and sometimes people won't embrace your ideas for change. This can pose a tremendous challenge for any leader.

But regardless of the burden that comes with being a change agent, there are steps you can take to lighten the load. In this chapter, you will learn the main reasons for resistance to change. This information can help you tackle the underlying causes of resistance so that you don't end up wasting time fighting useless battles. You will also explore how to show resolve, determination, and tenacity in the face of adversity. These traits are necessary for any leader who wants to implement change.

MAJOR REASONS FOR RESISTANCE TO CHANGE

There are certain aspects of leadership that you simply cannot avoid. For example, when you start a project, you're expected to see it through. You must have the resolve to drive the initiative to completion no matter how tough things get. Push hard on the critical issues and focus on the main goals. This requires a high level of resilience and the ability to adapt to changing circumstances.

A leader must maintain an optimistic mindset even when there's significant resistance from within and outside the organization. The good news is that leading change is a team effort. Though you may be the face of change, there are always people who can help you to weather the storms of adversity. But you need to be prepared to encourage and support your team to persevere through the challenges.

At the same time, you need to recognize that some employees are going to resist change. There are many reasons why they may do this. Employees working in the same organization may have different reasons for resisting change. By taking the time to understand these unique reasons, you stand a better chance of successfully driving the change initiative to completion. Here are the five biggest reasons why people resist change:

Potential for Job Loss

Whenever an organization decides to implement change, it is often aimed at enhancing structures, processes, and systems. Sometimes, these changes may mean fundamental adjustments, downsizing, or total elimination of specific job functions. In other words, some employees may find themselves facing demotions or job losses in the long or short term. This can lead to a groundswell of resistance from those who feel threatened by the change.

For example, if a new technology is being introduced, an employee may fear that the new system could lead to a lower position in the status hierarchy. When the system was manual, this employee was the focal point of that department. They felt powerful because everyone perceived them to be the go-to person whenever there was a problem. But now, this change is threatening to make them redundant or less powerful. The employee may decide to not learn or support this new system so that the company will keep relying on them. However, not every employee is malicious in their actions. Sometimes, the anxiety and self-doubt may be so crippling that they are unable to take action to support the change.

The organization may view change as an opportunity to improve efficiency, productivity, and profitability. A leader may think that change will have an overall benefit on many stakeholders. However, there are always casualties whenever a transformation occurs, and it's often the front-line workers who bear the brunt of it. Humans may be communal creatures, but they are also naturally self-serving. This means that those who feel their livelihoods are threatened will try their best to make the change process as difficult as possible. At the very least, they may decide not to actively support it.

Poor Communication and Engagement

George Bernard Shaw once said that the biggest problem in communication is assuming that it has taken place. Effective communication is a skill that anyone can learn, yet most people don't bother. It's easy to assume that your message has been well received simply because you put the information out there. However, your audience may have heard a very different message from what you said. Everyone in a leadership position must understand that effective communication acts as the bridge between clarity and confusion. When executing change in an organization, there's nothing as damaging as widespread confusion.

Poor communication can lead to change in opposition because employees may not fully understand what's happening. The way you communicate will determine how your employees react. You need to clearly articulate what needs to be changed and how the process will occur. You must also describe what the result will look like and the roles that employees are expected to play. If you fail to properly communicate all this, how do you expect people to jump on board to support you?

One of the main communication issues that often arise is a failure to explain the reason for the change. For example, you can't wake up one day and announce that the production system is being replaced by a new one.

If you don't explain that the new system is necessary and beneficial for all, you may experience a backlash. People who are used to the old system won't be convinced by a mere email or message board announcement. They will feel slighted by the lack of personal engagement. Some may even perceive the change to be some sort of punishment or a vendetta against them. While you may think that this is stretching things a bit too far, there are often a lot of underlying tensions within every organization. It's only during periods of transition that such tensions come to the forefront.

Lack of Trust

Every successful individual understands the value of trust, whether it's in personal or professional relation-ships. Where there is mutual trust, relationships flour-ish, and people work synergistically with unity of purpose. But in an environment where trust is lacking, resistance becomes the norm as people refuse to buy into each other's vision. In an organization, lack of trust could be the death knell for even the most positive endeavor.

But where does trust come from, and how is it broken?

Trust is gained through consistency of action and keeping your promises. It's about being true to your word, showing authentic kindness, and sticking to your values. Most importantly, trust is gained when you admit your mistakes openly and let others know that you've learned a lesson. The thing about trust is that you can't gain it overnight, but you can lose it in seconds.

As a leader, you make many commitments to people all the time. But if you fail to consistently keep your commitments without any explanation, people will stop trusting you. The same will happen if you're constantly flip-flopping between decisions. Your team may not say anything, but such traits do not go unnoticed. By the time you are launching a change process, very few will believe anything you say or do.

Let's face it. Sometimes, a leader may not be particularly well-liked by some employees. Of course, it's impossible to please everyone, especially when dealing with a large group of people. However, being liked and being trusted are two different things. People may not be fond of you on a personal level, but you better make sure that they trust in your leadership. Trust is about dependability — you being able to rely on your team and vice versa. If people don't trust you and your motivations, there won't be any collective progress when implementing change.

Uncertainty

We are living in uncertain times. Nobody knows for sure what the economic or political landscape will look like a year from now. Toss in the idea of introducing change in your organization, and you may create a tinderbox of anxiety and doubt. People are already on edge, and any notion of change may lead to resistance. The problem with uncertainty is that if it is unacceptable, it slowly turns into fear. Fear can be debilitating, and this is something you don't want when you are introducing change to an organization.

You may have communicated the change well and even explained that everyone's job is secure. Your team may trust your leadership. However, uncertainty is just part of life, and some people have a harder time dealing with it than others. Even a positive change, such as a promotion, can be received with anxiety as the employee contemplates their new responsibility. They may self-sabotage as a way to return to their previous, familiar role. In the same way, employees may sabotage a change process as a way of maintaining the familiarity of their workspace.

Poor Timing

Change may be resisted if it is introduced at the wrong time. For example, consider an organization that has just completed a massive change in its structure or hierarchy. Everyone is still recovering from the large-scale changes that have sent some individuals packing as others find themselves in unfamiliar roles. As CEO, you then decide that it's also a good time to overhaul your information management system.

Unfortunately, such back-to-back changes may be too much too soon for most people. They haven't even finished resisting the first change, and you already want to implement a new one? You may end up with a double backlash as even those who supported the first change decide to oppose the second one. It's not that the change is a bad idea, but the timing isn't right. People may resist as a way of telling you to slow things down.

It is important to identify the reasons why your employees are resisting change. Whatever the excuse may be, there are ways to resolve it.

OVERCOMING RESISTANCE TO CHANGE

Resistance to change can occur at several levels — organizational, group, and individual. Sometimes, an organization as a whole prefers to maintain the status quo. This often happens if employees are penalized for honest mistakes or if new ideas are not rewarded. Group resistance is often the result of trying to protect cohesive norms that define the group's identity. Any change that threatens to undermine this identity is likely to be resisted as members work to protect each other. Individual resistance is usually the result of fear, cultural background, or prior experiences. When you understand the level of resistance, you'll know how to deal with it in your organization. Here are nine ways to overcome resistance to change:

Directly Engage the Opposition

You have to directly engage with those who are resisting change. Your goal should be to find out what their concerns are and how to take care of them as quickly as possible. Don't try to bulldoze people who are opposed to change. Remember that they are still part of the organization, and it's better to have them complain in the open than sabotage in the background. By giving them a platform to provide their input, you're showing them that you value them and want them to be part of the team.

It's important to communicate early and as often as possible with employees. As a leader, you should ensure that communication channels are always open and active. Front-line employees need to be kept informed on what the organization is planning both in the present and future. You cannot put a price tag on honest and direct communication, especially when planning major changes at the workplace. Use available communication tools to inform your employees and receive their feedback. Company group chats, newsletters, and emails are all effective tools to use.

Honest communication is critical, especially when explaining why the change is needed. Try to show others how they will benefit from it and encourage them to support the change. When they can see the bigger picture and their role in it, they are less likely to resist change.

Listen and Respond to Feedback

Listening is a skill that is gradually dying out. In today's world, most people don't listen to gain a deeper understanding of the other person. People only pretend to listen as they wait to jump into the conversation with their opinion. This leads to a lack of effective engagement, and the other person may feel that you don't truly value their opinion. In an organization where employees don't feel heard or valued, they are likely to resist any kind of change.

As a leader, take the time to listen to your employees to receive and respond to their feedback. Your front-line workers are responsible for interacting with clients and keeping them happy daily. Therefore, they have a wealth of information that can help you ensure a smooth transition. Without proper consultation, any

186 | MARLENE GONZALEZ

change that affects their work performance is likely to be resisted.

You should arrange meetings with employees and ask them some probing questions. For example, "How do you feel about this change?", "How can we improve it?", and "What concerns do you have?". When employees respond, listen to what they are saying. If you cannot meet personally with employees, use engagement surveys to collect their feedback. The survey may even reveal more information than face-to-face meetings. Most employees are more comfortable providing anonymous responses with genuine feedback that may surprise you.

Depending on the feedback, make sure that it is used in adjusting the plan. This will show employees that you are serious about incorporating their opinions. It is also important to remember that in an organization, employees resist change for different reasons. Once you've identified these unique individual concerns, you should tailor your solutions to these problems appropriately.

Implement Change in Phases

As mentioned earlier, poor timing is one of the main reasons for resistance to change. People are likely to oppose change if too much is forced on them too soon.

You need to realize that change doesn't occur all at once. It's a process, not an event. Therefore, it's better to adopt a phased approach when making changes so that everyone has time to adapt to the transformations.

As a leader, the first phase should always involve preparations. Announce the change to all stakeholders and be ready for feedback. Use it to create a plan, then share it across the organization. The goal is to prepare people psychologically to embrace change. The next phase is to take action and design a change management plan. Use your change champions to disseminate the plan to the front-line workers. During this phase, your goal should be to ensure that change is executed according to the plan. In the final phase, monitor the change to ensure that people follow through on it. The goal is to support the change and keep people from going back to the old way of doing things.

Practice Effective Communication

Effective communication is critical at every stage of the change process. Stakeholders need to be kept in the loop, and therefore, you must explicitly communicate with them about what's going on. You can combine formal and informal communication methods to ensure that the message is received by as many people as possible. Individuals tend to have preferences when it comes to modes of communication. While some prefer emails and newsletters, others may be more comfortable with face-to-face meetings and town halls. Therefore, you should employ a wide range of communication channels to explain the vision of change, and everyone's expected role in its implementation.

Connect the Change to Pertinent Issues

In an organization, senior management usually has an agenda that it wants to be implemented. Senior executives are often concerned with the overarching vision and how to execute such goals. These goals are then broken down and shared with lower levels in the organizational hierarchy. However, mid-level and front-line employees also have their concerns. They have issues that dominate their minds, for example, job security. Just because they are tasked with implementing the organizational goals doesn't mean their concerns go away. If they feel that the change goes against their interests, they will oppose it.

This can pose a major problem for a change leader. How do you ensure that change is implemented without alienating the issues that people care about? The best solution is to link the change to whatever concerns employees have. If they are worried about job security, show them how the change will help secure it. If they are concerned about long working hours, explain to them how the change is connected to improved efficiency and a lighter workload.

Don't make things up or lie to your employees just to get them to support the change. Imagine what would happen if you made false promises, and they later found out that you were not truthful. Be genuine when showing them how change is aligned with the issues they care about. This also ensures that they won't abandon the change when new concerns arise in the future.

Show Empathy to Employee Concerns

Empathy goes a long way in forging the kind of connections needed to drive change from planning to full adoption. Empathy goes beyond listening to what someone is saying. It is tapping into the other person's intentions and emotional state. It involves paying attention, accepting others' different opinions, and appreciating their feedback. The best way to show that you care and understand their concerns is to communicate the change right from the start. Even as you contemplate why change is necessary and what form it will take, you should be actively collecting the views of your employees.

Open communication channels, and let others know about the change initiative. Ask them to explain their core concerns rather than just the surface-level issues they have. By accepting and appreciating their candor without judgment, you are creating a way to influence them later on. Valuing their concerns makes it less likely for them to resist change.

Identify Your Change Supporters

There are two sides to every coin. As much as some resist change, there is another group that supports it. You need to identify those who support change and use them as advocates for the new way of doing things. The supporters and the resisters are peers who work together and probably know each other personally. They speak the same language and understand each other's concerns better than you do. Once you've sold the idea of change to the supporters, send them out to convince those who are resisting. Provide them with a platform and opportunity to participate in forums to help get the message out.

Be Transparent

Change is synonymous with uncertainty, and uncertainty usually creates a sense of loss of control. Nobody likes to feel powerless when it comes to controlling their outcomes. When someone doesn't feel in control, they become stressed and suspicious of everything around them. Employees may become suspicious of the change initiative and assume the worst possible scenario.

To avoid this, you must have open and transparent conversations with your team. Give them as much information as possible to ensure a high level of certainty. Tell them what the change is about and what steps will be taken to implement it. You should also clarify the aspects of their work that will change and those that won't be affected. For those decisions that haven't been defined yet, ask for employee input. By being as transparent as possible with information, you are giving them a semblance of control over the process. They don't have to worry or guess about what's going to happen next because they have the details.

Provide Resources

If you want your team to embrace change as quickly as possible, you must prepare them before and during the transition period. Offer training classes and tools that can help them adapt to the change. By providing such resources, you also enable them to hit the ground running in the new environment. Ensure that the resources are still available after the change in case they need a refresher course. By empowering your team, you minimize the risk of resistance and also encourage them to look forward to the future.

TIPS FOR MANAGING RESISTANCE TO CHANGE

In the previous section, you learned some steps you can take to overcome resistance to change. Overcoming resistance to change in an organization requires tactfulness and practicality. You need to have the right mindset and a plan that others can buy into. Your employees must see you as a competent and considerate leader. The way you handle the issues around the change initiative will determine whether they trust your intentions for change. With that said, here are five more tips on how to manage resistance to change:

Take the Right Approach from the Start

You can avoid resistance to change by simply taking the right approach from the early stages of the change cycle. There's no need to wait for the opposition to arise before taking action. Design a change management plan that makes employees enthusiastic and engaged in the change initiative. From the moment the change project is initiated, you should have a structured approach to managing every aspect of change. Senior leaders must be seen actively supporting and communicating the need for change to employees. You should also recruit mid-level managers and front-line supervisors to advocate for change at all levels.

Expect Resistance

Studies on the brain show that resistance to change is a physiological reaction. The brain prefers to maintain the status quo as a way of preserving energy. Therefore, you shouldn't be surprised when some people oppose your change initiative. Even though the change may be a solution to a problem, some employees will still struggle to support it. Accept resistance to change as normal and focus on how to mitigate it before launching the change project.

The best place to start is by exploring the likeliest sources of resistance in your organization. The major sources of resistance are usually those employees who have invested a lot of time and energy in the current way of doing things. It could be a manager who created the current system and may not want to see any changes made to it. Resistance could also come from people who had a different idea of what the change should look like.

There are many cases where a project team acknowledges that they knew there would be resistance from a particular source, yet they didn't do anything about it. Once you've identified where the strongest resistance is likely to come from, find out why. Be proactive and take necessary action ahead of time before this resistance gets out of control.

Create a Formal Process to Manage Resistance

You shouldn't be scrambling to manage resistance to change. If you are, then you have failed to create an effective change management plan. There are several strategies you can adopt as part of a formal process to manage resistance. These strategies can be condensed into three steps.

The first step is to prepare for change. Assess potential points of resistance and identify tactics to mitigate them. Secondly, manage the change by creating a resistance management plan. This plan should address any obstacles that may hinder the success of the change initiative. The third step is to reinforce the change. This involves collecting feedback to understand any concerns employees may still have after adopting the change. Evaluate this feedback to identify how to close any pending gaps in compliance with the new system.

Pinpoint the Underlying Causes of Resistance

When implementing change, you are likely to detect some overt forms of resistance from employees. For example, you may notice a lot of complaining, failing to attend important meetings, ignoring a request for information, or simply refusing to comply with a new process. As a leader, you may try to force people to change these behaviors, but ultimately, you're only dealing with the symptoms of the problem. To effectively manage resistance, you must identify its root causes. Focus on finding out *why* someone is resistant rather than *how* they are resisting.

Some of the root causes of resistance include:

- Failure of the leadership to explain why the change is being made
- Fear of losing one's job
- How the organization handled a previous change
- Poor commitment and support from managers

Once you've diagnosed and understood the root causes, you should tackle the biggest cause first. By dealing with the lack of awareness of why change is being made, you can quickly resolve the rest of the underlying issues.

Identify the Right Resistance Managers

When dealing with resistance to change, you cannot leave this task to your change management team or human resources department. The best resistance managers are usually senior leaders, mid-level managers, and front-line supervisors. Senior leadership is best positioned to explain the need for change and provide visible support for change. If senior leaders don't show overt commitment, employees will deem the change to be insignificant.

Managers and supervisors work closely with front-line employees. They know their employees on a more personal level than senior leaders do. Their enthusiasm and commitment to change can inspire their subordinates to wholly embrace change. If this group appears cold toward change, employees will react in the same way. Therefore, make sure that there is no resistance from managers and supervisors before requesting them to become resistance managers.

Though you may want the change process to be smooth, there is always going to be some kind of resistance. Even your most loyal team members may not support change. However, you should understand what the reasons for resistance are and find the best strategies for overcoming it.

KEY TAKEAWAYS

When implementing change in an organization, you want your employees to support your ideas. You need to engage them thoroughly so that they don't become stumbling blocks to your intended change. Here are five strategies to boost employee engagement as a way of overcoming resistance to change:

1. *Be clear in explaining how their work performance impacts the organization's success.* Start by discussing organizational goals with employees and ask for their input to create a sense of ownership. Once all parties understand the reasoning behind the goals, assign priorities for individuals and teams. Review the goals quarterly rather than annually to maintain realistic expectations. Continually monitor and update goals using a centralized system so everyone can keep track of them.

2. *Offer opportunities for personal development.* Millennials love personal development to improve their skills and quality of life. Create affinity groups where employees come together to assess each other's strengths and weaknesses. These groups also provide opportunities to cross-train, so colleagues learn new skills. You can offer employees discounts at the nearby gym to improve their physical fitness. You can also provide opportunities to further their education, such as online courses, conferences, and tuition reimbursement.

3. *Develop and invest in your managers.* Provide managers with tools, such as employee engagement software and 360-degree feedback, to help them collect relevant data. Train them

on how to identify and analyze trends among different demographics within your team. Encourage managers to sit down with employees and have open conversations about what improvements need to be made and how to do it. By keeping managers informed and engaged, you teach them to do the same with their subordinates.

4. *Re-recruit your employees.* Instead of constantly looking for new talent, regularly check in on your employees to assess their happiness with the organization. Schedule one-on-one team meetings to discuss progress, voice concerns, and update goals. Meetings should be held weekly, monthly, or quarterly depending on your schedule. Share the agenda in advance to ensure everyone comes prepared. Treat these meetings as a coaching session with open conversations rather than a lecture. Create follow-up steps to ensure all parties are held accountable for their commitments.

5. *Create a culture of employee appreciation.* Set aside time at the end of the Friday workday to host an appreciation meeting. During the meeting, employees can step forward and recognize colleagues for their contribution to the team. You can also have monthly lunch parties where

the company pays for food and brings together employees to celebrate. Leaders can recognize birthdays and service anniversaries on social media, thanking employees for their contribution to the organization. You can also give awards to individuals or teams that have the greatest impact on the organization's annual goals.

8

LEADING CHANGE AND PUTTING IT ALL TOGETHER

Research shows that organizations are struggling to keep pace with the changes occurring all over the world. This rapid rate of change will only increase over time. Leaders must get the attention of major stakeholders and communicate the need for rapid changes to the status quo. Therefore, you should create a sense of urgency in your organization to avoid being left behind.

Creating a sense of urgency is important because you need the cooperation of all relevant stakeholders. You must convince them that the status quo is dangerous and there's greater value in transforming the organization. Have an honest conversation with them about the current market, available opportunities, potential crises, and competitive realities. Once you have created a sense of urgency, you should take the following 6 steps of change management. These steps will help you assess, prepare, plan, and execute your change initiative. Here are the 6 steps of leading any kind of change, anywhere and at any time:

1. **Develop a vision** – Ask your employees to imagine the positive outcomes of the change. Use visual aids such as PowerPoint presentations to help them see the benefits the change will have on their work. This will inspire them to create their own compelling vision of what the ideal future will look like.

2. **Communicate the change vision** – Develop a communication plan that inspires urgency and encourages people to buy into your change vision. Use multiple communication channels such as discussion groups, newsletters, and one-on-one meetings to communicate the change vision.

3. **Create a coalition** – Build a coalition of trusted allies who will support you in implementing the change. Ensure that this core coalition is spread out across all levels of the organization.

4. **Empower your team** – Provide your team with

the training and tools they need to successfully implement the change. Use tools such as checklists, refresher courses, and regular reminders to help them stay on track. You can also use rewards to encourage those who support the change.

5. **Generate short-term wins** – Allocate resources to meeting short-term milestones. When you achieve a milestone, celebrate it no matter how small it may seem. This encourages people to move on to the next milestone and eliminates any lingering doubt about implementing the change.

6. **Embed new approaches into the culture** – Promote norms and values that are aligned to the change by hiring individuals who fit the new norms. You can also reward those who are supporting the new norms and reassign or fire those who are still resisting the change.

CHANGE WIZARD: FINAL TAKEAWAYS

Chapter 1: Why the Need for Change?

- *There are five main reasons why every organization should embrace change:* rapid technological changes, global economic changes, the evolution of customer desires, the need for continuous upgrading of employee skills, and the need for innovation.

- *There are a lot of changes occurring in the business world right now.* Most of these changes are taking place in four key areas: the adoption of remote work, the transformation of physical offices, reduced business travel, and the acceleration of digital transformation.

- *The most visible change in the world today is accelerated digitization.* The three main benefits of embracing digital changes are increased revenue, improved efficiency, and identification of growth opportunities.

- *You need to use the right strategies to adapt to the changing trends.* You should leverage the available technological solutions to enhance business communication. Stay optimistic to inspire your team to be resilient in adversity. Finally, prepare your organization for the new normal by consulting widely and focusing on the bigger picture.

Chapter 2: Appreciate Diversity and the Role of Politics

- *Enhancing cultural awareness makes collaboration easier when working to achieve a collective goal.* There are practical steps you can take to create cultural awareness. You can establish policies that appreciate diversity and train employees to be global citizens. Celebrate cultural holidays from around the world and learn about different traditions. You should also promote clear communication and practice good manners to avoid misunderstandings among people of diverse backgrounds. It also helps to pay attention to foreign colleagues and customers, especially if they live in different time zones.
- *A leader must have strong political skills.* To develop good political skills at the workplace, you need to excel in four major areas: networking, sincerity, social astuteness, and interpersonal influence.
- *Some people are not naturally endowed with political skills, but there are steps you can take to improve them.* You can practice mindfulness, develop social skills, build strong networks, learn effective communication skills, practice transparency and assertiveness, and avoid political arguments.

- *Office politics are inevitable.* You can survive them by assessing where the real power lies in your organization. You should work to understand the informal network, create your own, and use it to build your profile. Develop strong interpersonal skills and try to understand those who engage in dirty politics as a way to learn to defuse negative politics.

Chapter 3: Challenge the Status Quo

- *Questioning the status quo helps in preventing complacency.* It also enables you to see and grab opportunities as they arise.
- *Leaders often fear challenging the status quo for five reasons:* fear of accountability, risk aversion, ignorance of how to implement change, lack of organizational readiness, and failure to evolve in leadership.
- *To challenge the status quo, you must learn to ask the right questions.* You need to prioritize your ideas, recruit allies, and work on your pitch. You should also be patient and consult others. Ask a lot of questions and be bold in exploring all avenues.

Chapter 4: Design a Change Management Process

- Change management refers to *the process of leading organizational change from conception, through implementation, and finally to resolution.*
- *There are three types of organizational changes:* adaptive, transformative, and fundamental changes. Adaptive changes refer to tiny and iterative adjustments made by an organization to improve processes, strategies, and products over time. Transformational changes refer to bigger changes that have a wider scope and signify a sudden or monumental shift from the status quo. Fundamental changes are large-scale unpredictable shifts that affect the entire organization and take years to implement.
- *There are five key steps in change management.* The first step is preparation. The second step is creating a plan that includes strategic goals, KPIs. and a scope. The third is implementing and embedding the change and finally reviewing the progress and results.

Chapter 5: Apply the 10 Principles of Change Management

- *Stability is important for an organization to stay*

focused and productive. Leaders must adapt quickly to changing market conditions. They must focus not only on strategic plans but also on the human aspect of change management as well.

- *A leader should thoroughly address issues that affect their employees when creating a change management plan.* This can be done in group discussions or at the individual level. By clearly articulating the case for change and listening to their employees, you can maintain morale and ensure timely adoption of the change.

- *During times of transition, a leader should lead from the front to create unity of purpose and ensure collaboration.* They must involve every level of the organization during the planning phase. This ensures that teams from different departments take ownership of the change initiative.

- *The message of change needs to be communicated clearly and regularly through multiple channels.* This ensures that as many employees as possible understand and embrace the change initiative.

- *Before implementing change, you must understand the existing organizational culture.* This information can help you when designing the various elements of change. If you feel that the existing culture must change, then explain to your employees how adopting a new culture will be more effective in achieving organizational goals.

Chapter 6: Be Decisive and Tough-minded

- *To be decisive means to be firm, resolute, and determined.* A tough-minded individual has a strong will and doesn't change their mind easily once it's made up. Embracing both qualities will earn you the respect of your team. You are viewed as a leader who quickly marshals the troops to come up with ideas, chooses the best one, and then follows through on it.

- *Good leaders perceive decision-making as a process rather than an event.* This process has seven steps: gathering information, encouraging constructive conflict, considering different opinions, not imposing your ideas, testing assumptions, explaining your decisions, and staying engaged during implementation.

- *To make decisions faster, you must learn to trust your gut and think about the bigger picture.* You should also limit the information and use visual aids to help process information. Act as if you're advising a friend to avoid making emotional decisions.

- *A decisive leader has three qualities.* They are confident, resistant to change, and hold themselves accountable.
- *A collaborative leader takes their time before making a decision.* They also encourage feedback from others and consult those with opposing views. Finally, they understand their impact as a decision-maker.

Chapter 7: Maintain Drive and Persistence

- *People resist change for five main reasons:* fear of job loss, lack of trust, poor communication from leaders, uncertainty, and poor timing of the change.
- *You can overcome resistance to change by directly engaging those who oppose it and responding to their feedback.* You should also implement change in phases and practice effective communication. Connect the change to pertinent issues and show empathy to employee concerns. You need to identify your change supporters, provide them with resources, and be transparent with your team.
- *To manage resistance, take the right approach from*

the start by creating a resistance management plan. Resistance is inevitable, so work to find its underlying causes. When you do, identify the right resistance managers to disseminate information to front-line workers.

CONCLUSION

As humans, we love to stay in our comfort zones. We see this every day with people choosing to follow the same old habits and patterns. It's okay to have a healthy aversion to risk. This is how we have survived as a species for eons. But there is a limit to what you can achieve by staying in your comfort zone. At some point, you realize that change is inevitable, and it is not your enemy. Change is simply a way of helping you transform into something better so that you can move onto that next level. Think of a situation where a pawn on a chessboard refuses to move forward out of fear. It may survive longer, but at what cost? A pawn may become a queen if it gets to the back line on the opponent's side. By refusing to change position, it sacrifices the possibility of being transformed into a more valuable piece.

This book has clearly explained to you how the business landscape is changing at an incredibly fast pace. As a leader, you cannot afford to be left behind. Rest assured that the leadership in other organizations is paying attention to these changes, and they are planning how to take full advantage of them. You have also learned the importance of maintaining cultural and political awareness in your organization. By appreciating the diversity in culture among your workforce, you create greater understanding and more cohesiveness in your team. Like it or not, every organization has its internal politics. You need to have political skills so you can use your networks to implement the changes you want.

Challenging the status quo is easier said than done. You've learned some great tips on how to do this as a way to accelerate change. But keep in mind that every leader has their unique approach to change. Your goal should be to use this information to find a strategy that works for you. Therefore, take the information in this book and use it in a way that fits your unique goals and perspective.

The content in this book is very practical and you can use it as you wish to design your own unique change process. You may adjust some of the details depending on what you want to achieve in your organization.

However, follow the fundamental principles explained in this book. They will guide you along the way.

As you follow these guidelines, do stay open-minded and adaptable when challenging the status quo so that you don't get stuck during the process. Part of this process involves assessing whether your organization is ready for change. A leader needs to provide a vision for the future, and this means designing a change process that guides the organization during the transition period. Use the principles of change management provided in this book to help you create a plan that is effective and collaborative.

You will run into resistance to change, and you must be prepared for all kinds of opposition. You have to be decisive and tough-minded to achieve your goals because some of your decisions will be unpopular. You have learned some key techniques on how to make decisions faster and not get swayed by different opinions. These strategies can help you become a collaborative decision-maker who shows resolve and determination when faced with resistance. At the end of the day, you must understand the underlying sources of resistance to change. Once you do so, you stand a better chance of convincing your employees to support change for the benefit of the organization.

In today's world, a leader must constantly be preparing for the future. You must be ready to challenge the way you do things and take steps to adapt to whatever situation may arise. If you don't, you will lose your competitive edge. You don't want your organization to be the next Kodak or Blackberry.

See your organization as a living being that constantly needs refreshing to keep it vibrant and productive. Why settle for anything less? You now have the tools to shift your mindset and set your organization on the path of positive transformation. Will you choose change or stagnation? The time for action is now.

Dear Reader,

I hope you like it!

As a self-publishing author, I rely on readers like you to help promote my work and serve humanity better by doing my best to write, share, coach and train the next generation of leaders like you.

Please, consider posting an online review on Amazon, a short review, audio, or a picture highlighting the page you enjoyed the most. Book reviews are essential to any book. They help potential buyers make confident decisions when getting and buying books.

www.amazon.com/review/create-review/
asim=B09DTJXLVJ/

Unlock the leader in you.

Your coach, Marlene Gonzalez.

ABOUT THE AUTHOR

Marlene Gonzalez is the founder and the president of Life coaching group LLC. focusing on Leadership development and executive coaching. She passionately pursues one vision- "To advance, develop and promote minority leaders." She is a renowned executive coach and facilitator. She is the author of the coaching series Leadership Wizard; "Number 1 New Release book in the Education and Leadership category". Her book series specializes in transformational leadership topics such as:

- *Leadership Wizard. The Nine Dimensions. Unlock the Leader in You. The Discipline of Coaching Yourself to Fearlessly Lead, Influence, Inspire and Empower Others.*

- *Assertive Wizard. How To Boost Confidence, Get Your Message Across, And Speak With Impact.*
- *Change Wizard. Master The Art Of Leading Change And Working Together for a Common Purpose.*
- *Confident Wizard.* Turn Self Doubt Into Confidence: The Ultimate Guide To Lead With Authenticity, Purpose, and Resilience.

Once you master these and many other topics she covers, you can transform your life and become a more successful leader. In addition, you will find that her books have a straight-to-the-point approach and easy to implement actions. She is passionate about sharing her insights and resources on transformational leadership through a combination of Insights Discovery, the psychology of C. G. Jung, her corporate career experience and her professional coaching expertise.

González held many executive corporate positions in the US, Europe, and Latin America. She is the former Senior Director of Global Training, Learning, and Development for McDonald's Corporation. Marlene holds a BS, an Executive MBA/PAG, and a graduate diploma on managerial Issues in the global enterprise from Thunderbird University. www.marlenegonzalez.com

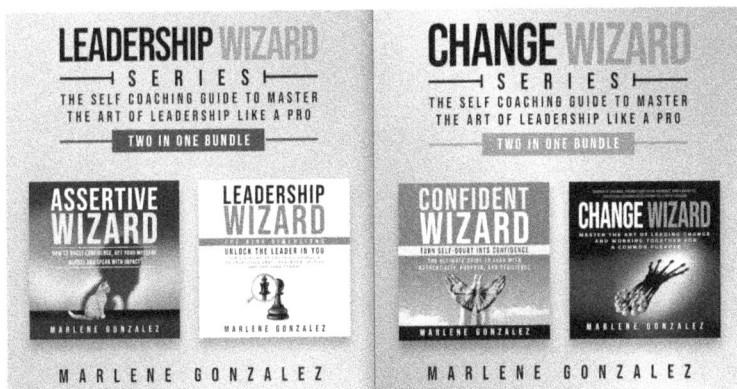

REFERENCES

Achor, S. & Gielan, M. (July 4, 2020). What leading with optimism really looks like. *Harvard Business Review.* Retrieved from https://hbr.org/2020/06/what-leading-with-optimism-really-looks-like

Aguirre, D., Calderone, M. & Jones, J. (2004). 10 principles of change management: Tools and techniques to help companies transform quickly. Retrieved from https://www.strategy-business.com/article/rr00006?gko=dab72

Ahmed, A. (July 02, 2020). Culture awareness in the workplace. Retrieved from https://smallbusiness.chron.com/practices-could-implement-increase-cultural-sensitivity-acceptance-workplace-16661.html

Bart, C. & McQueen, G. (2013). Why women make better directors. *International Journal of Business Governance and Ethics*, 2013; 8 (1): 93 DOI: 10.1504/IJBGE.2013.052743

Belsky, G. (February 18, 2017). Sincerity as a leadership trait. *LinkedIn*. https://www.linkedin.com/pulse/sincerity-leadership-trait-george-belsky

Business News Daily. (February 27, 2020). Want to be a better leader? Build your political skills. Retrieved from https://www.businessnewsdaily.com/9465-political-skills-happiness.html

DeakinCo. (22 September, 2017). *Seven practices you can implement to increase cultural awareness in the workplace.* Retrieved from https://www.deakinco.com/media-centre/news/seven-practices-you-can-implement-to-increase-cultural-awareness-in-the-workplace.

Freifeld, L. (May 15, 2013). Interpersonal networking skills make leaders more effective: 8 critical skills needed for effective social networking. *Training Mag.* Retrieved from https://trainingmag.com/interpersonal-networking-skills-make-leaders-more-effective/

Galvin, J. (2021). The climb to recovery continues. *Vistage*. Retrieved from https://www.vistage.com/research-center/business-financials/economic-trends/20201020-the-climb-to-recovery-continues/

Gartner Inc. (2019). Successful organizational change management: Reality or aspiration? Retrieved from https://www.gartner.com/en/human-resources/insights/organizational-change-management

Gino, F. (October 24, 2016). Let your workers rebel. Retrieved from https://hbr.org/2016/10/let-your-workers-rebel

Hire Success. Indecisive vs. decisive personality traits. Retrieved from https://www.hiresuccess.com/help/indecisive-vs-decisive-personality-types-at-work. Accessed on July 2, 2021.

Holst, A. (June 16, 2020). Blackberry – Statistics and facts. Statista. Retrieved from https://www.statista.com/topics/5316/blackberry/#topicHeader__wrapper.

Insights. Dealing with resistance to change. Retrieved from https://www.insights.com/resources/dealing-with-resistance-to-change/

Mencl, Wefald, A. & Ittersum, K. (July 4, 2016). Transformational leader attributes: Interpersonal skills, engagement, and well-being. *Leadership & Organization Development Journal ISSN: 0143-7739.* Retrieved from https://www.emerald.com/insight/content/doi/10.1108/LODJ-09-2014-0178/full/html?skipTracking=true

McMaster University. (March 26, 2013). Study says women make better decisions for companies than men. Retrieved from https://phys.org/news/2013-03-women-decisions-companies-men.html

Miller, K. (March 19, 2020). 5 critical steps in the change management process. *Harvard Business School Online*. Retrieved from https://online.hbs.edu/blog/post/change-management-process

Mirza, B. (September 25, 2019). Toxic workplace cultures hurt workers and company profits. *SHRM*. Retrieved from https://www.shrm.org/resourcesandtools/hr-topics/employee-relations/pages/toxic-workplace-culture-report.aspx

Ojala, S. & Pyoria, P. (August 16, 2017). Mobile knowledge workers and traditional mobile workers: Assessing the prevalence of multi-locational work in Europe. Retrieved from https://journals.sagepub.com/doi/full/10.1177/0001699317722593

Paycor. (July 17, 2019). Overcoming employee resistance to change in the workplace. Retrieved from https://www.paycor.com/resource-center/articles/overcoming-employee-resistance-to-change-in-the-workplace/

Resume Labs. (2021). Remote work and telecommuting statistics for 2021. Retrieved from https://resumelab.-

com/job-search/remote-work-statistics

Shi, J., Chen, Z. & Zhou, L. (2011). Testing differential mediation effects of sub-dimensions of political skills in linking proactive personality to employee performance. *J Bus Psychol* 26, 359–369. Retrieved from https://doi.org/10.1007/s10869-010-9195-0

SHRM. *Navigating Covid-19: The next chapter of work.* Retrieved from https://pages.shrm.org/next-chapter-economic-index?
_ga=2.24738874.145361710.1589385259-1522955478.1545034942

Vetter, A. (Sep 14, 2018). How to be a stronger and faster decision maker. *Inc* . Retrieved from https://www.inc.com/amy-vetter/how-to-be-more-decisive-when-making-major-business-decisions.html

Vistage CEO Confidence Index (June 2020). *Economic optimism among small and midsize businesses in Q2 matches 2008 recession.* Retrieved from https://www.vistage.com/research-center/wp-content/uploads/2020/06/CI-flyer-Q220-2.pdf

Wilson, C. (Jun 14, 2018). Trusting your gut is the best business tool you've got—if you can listen. Retrieved from https://www.forbes.com/sites/chipwilson/2018/06/14/trusting-your-gut-is-the-best-business-tool-youve-got-if-you-can-listen/

World Economic Forum. (January 2016). The future of jobs employment, skills and workforce strategy for the fourth industrial revolution. Retrieved from http://www3.weforum.org/docs/WEF_FOJ_Executive_Summary_Jobs.pdf

World Economic Forum, Global Competitiveness Report (2020). https://www.weforum.org/reports/the-global-competitiveness-report-2020

Zielenziger, D. (2011). The final 'Kodak moment': 5 reasons why bankruptcy would be tragic. *International Business Times*. Retrieved from https://www.ibtimes.com/final-kodak-moment-5-reasons-why-bankruptcy-would-be-tragic-320644

www.ingramcontent.com/pod-product-compliance
Lightning Source LLC
Chambersburg PA
CBHW021617270326
41931CB00008B/743